Hilda of Whitby

Published by
The Bible Reading Fellowship
15 The Chambers, Vineyard
Abingdon OX14 3FE
United Kingdom
Tel: +44 (0)1865 319700
Email: enquiries@brf.org.uk
Website: www.brf.org.uk
BRF is a Registered Charity

ISBN 978 1 84101 728 0

First published 2014
Reprinted 2014 (twice), 2016
10 9 8 7 6 5 4 3
All rights reserved

Acknowledgments
Unless otherwise stated, scripture quotations are taken from The New Revised Standard
Version of the Bible, Anglicised edition, copyright © 1989, 1995 by the Division of
Christian Education of the National Council of the Churches of Christ in the United States
of America, and are used by permission. All rights reserved.

Scripture quotations from The Revised Standard Version of the Bible, copyright © 1946,
1952, 1971 by the Division of Christian Education of the National Council of the Churches
of Christ in the United States of America, are used by permission. All rights reserved.

Extracts from the Authorised Version of the Bible (The King James Bible), the rights in
which are vested in the Crown, are reproduced by permission of the Crown's Patentee,
Cambridge University Press.

p. 39: Lyrics from *Columba: A play with music* by Juliet Boobbyer and Joanna Sciortino
reprinted by kind permission of Gracewing.

p. 98: Hymn lyrics reprinted by kind permission of June Boyce-Tillman.

pp. 100, 105–106: Extracts from Ray Simpson, *The Celtic Prayer Book Vol. 4: Great Celtic
Christians* (Kevin Mayhew, 2004), reprinted by permission of Kevin Mayhew

Cover images: (Whitby front) John Dowie/Flickr/Gettyimages; (Whitby back) Istockphoto/
Thinkstock; (Cross) Istockphoto/Thinkstock

Every effort has been made to trace and contact copyright owners for material used in
this resource. We apologise for any inadvertent omissions or errors, and would ask those
concerned to contact us so that full acknowledgment can be made in the future.

A catalogue record for this book is available from the British Library

Printed and bound by CPI Group (UK) Ltd, Croydon CR0 4YY

Hilda of Whitby

A spirituality for now

Ray Simpson

Note

Anglo-Saxon names were spelt in various ways. In this book I have used prevalent modern English spelling for lead names such as Hilda (rather than Hild), Enfleda (rather than Aenflaed) and Elfleda (rather than Aelflaed). Some written and online sources use the more exact spellings.

Hilda's father, Hereric, was a nephew of King Edwin, which means that Hilda was Edwin's great-niece. For simplicity's sake, however, I sometimes refer to them as uncle and niece.

I quote often from the Venerable Bede's Ecclesiastical History of the English People, *usually from the Oxford University Press World Classics edition (1994) or the Penguin Classics edition (1990). Where possible, I give a page number from the book rather than directing the reader to the endnotes.*

Contents

Family tree of Hilda

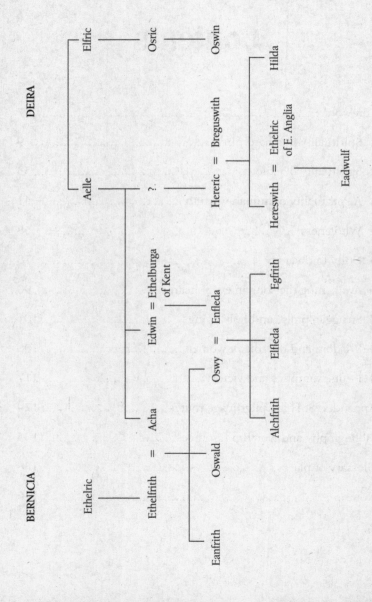

Foreword

We have much to be thankful for in God's own county, but of all the bright stars of Yorkshire's rich heritage of Christian witness, for me St Hilda of Whitby shines out as one of the brightest. I am thankful to Ray Simpson for retelling her story in a way that connects so directly with our contemporary world, inspiring prayer and reflection which I trust will bear fruit as it did so abundantly, graciously and quietly in her own life.

I enjoy my visits to Whitby, not just for the fantastic kippers I often come away with, but also because Hilda's memory lives on in the faith, hope and love of today's Christian community in that town. I thank God also that the Sisters of the Order of the Holy Paraclete continue the monastic tradition in that town, with their Mother House, St Hilda's Priory, Sneaton Castle, looking across the bay to the ruins of the abbey where Hilda's church once stood.

Hilda's example of self-sacrificial leadership, and of courageous acceptance of what the gathered church discerned as the will of God, is a particular challenge to us today. At the Synod of Whitby over which she presided, although she was a firm believer in the Celtic way she accepted fundamental changes to the time-honoured ecclesiastical polity of the Celtic church. She was willing to embrace the new ways of the Roman mission for the sake of the unity of the Church's witness in this land.

Hilda was baptised on Easter Day, 12 April 627, on the site where York Minster stands today, along with King Edwin, by Paulinus, first Bishop of York. In recent years I have baptised new believers on the same spot outside the Minster, along with other local church leaders. I visited Hinderwell a few months after becoming Archbishop of York. I baptised a baby at Hilda's well and drank water from the well too!

My prayer is that those baptised today, and all of us who seek to follow Jesus in the north of England, will follow Hilda's example. With her I hope we shall live wholeheartedly for Jesus, carrying the light of God into the communities to which we belong, and seeing the love of God transform both church and nation.

This book will help us along the way.

+Sentamu Eboracencis

Spirituality in a hard place

When the English nation was being formed,
when the people's gods lost their shine
and the true God began to loom large;
when its church was like a chrysalis emerging from its Irish womb
but did not yet know how to fly—
God placed a shining woman on a throne not made by man
at the centre of two worlds no one else could span.
Her name was Hilda.

In spring, when 'God's in his heaven—all's right with the world' (Robert Browning, 'Pippa's song'), people usually exude good spirit. When they are in a hard place, however, the spirit of complaint can all too easily take over. Hilda was born in a hard place. Her family were pagans and her people were brutal. While she was still in her mother's womb, her father fled for his life and died by poisoning. Her mother, Breguswith, had to rear two daughters bereft of her home and her husband. Many of us, born into such a situation, would grow up resentful and inward-looking; Hilda grew up caring and outgoing. The ousted ruling family of the Anglo-Saxon kingdom of Deira, into which she was born, loved power obtained by violence; she empowered people through love. What was the secret of her transformation? How can so generous a spirituality grow in such a hard place?

Hilda was born in 614 in the eastern part of a Britain that was being colonised by hardened Anglo-Saxons. In other parts of the country, the original Celtic Britons, fiery and fractious though they could be, had been introduced to Christ, the Son of the one true God. Across the sea, Ireland had become a land of saints and scholars. Christian missionaries had established hundreds of 'villages of God', seven-days-a-week communities of prayer and work, serviced by monks, nuns, the local people and the spiritual foster mothers who welcomed people with open hearts. It was now the turn of the Anglo-Saxons to discover fresh gleams of light. Who were they, and how did they discover this 'something more'?

Germanic men began to arrive in longboats on Britain's southern shores before the last Roman troops left in 410. They continued to arrive while Britain's fratricidal Celtic kingdoms strove to reassert themselves. They included Angles, Saxons, Frisians and Jutes. Roman-trained British chiefs employed them as mercenaries and ceded to them certain territories, but the Saxons mutinied because they were not paid their wages, and battles ensued.[1] The Saxons were defeated in a major battle at Mount Badon around AD500, but, after that, things swung their way. These aristocratic male warriors were comparatively few in proportion to the indigenous population, but they captured the hilltop garrisons, slew the tribal leaders and extended their rule over the Celtic population. Tom Holland writes that 'European historians have traditionally seen the arrival of the Franks in the land that would eventually become France, and of the Angles in the future England, as events of far greater long-term significance than the activities of the Caesar of Rome or the Persian King'[2]— that is, of the Roman and Persian empires.

By the early seventh century, Kent and East Anglia were the leading Anglo-Saxon kingdoms. Kent's king, Ethelbert, took a wife from the Franks, Bertha, who was a Christian. In 590, her husband welcomed Augustine and the mission from Italy sent by Pope Gregory. King Redwald came to the East Anglian throne some three years later and adopted Christianity. He had difficulty in persuading his people to follow his new religion, and perhaps he himself 'halted between two opinions' (1 Kings 18:21, KJV), for he maintained a temple with altars to both pagan and Christian gods.

The other Anglo-Saxons remained stubbornly pagan. From about 450 they gradually spread west and north. Aelle defeated the Britons and colonised land in the Yorkshire Wolds, just to the north of the Humber, in a land they called Deira. He was its first Saxon king. Hilda's father, Prince Hereric, was a nephew of Aelle's son, Edwin. Hereric married Breguswith when he became old enough to be a warrior, and they had their first daughter, Hereswith.

The Angles colonised lowland river valleys of the north-eastern coast, such as the Tyne, Wear and Tees. It is possible that a group of Angles from Lincolnshire (a region then known as Lindis feorna, later Lindsey) colonised the Bamburgh area on the north-east coast and named the nearby island Lindisfarne. Certainly in 547 the coastal stronghold of Bamburgh was seized by the Angle chief Ida the Flame-bearer, who became king of that region in 560; the region became known as Bernicia. Some of the remaining Celtic kingdoms in the north saw his successor, Theodoric, as weak, and in 575 they besieged him on Lindisfarne (known to the Celts as Medcaut, 'island of healing'). Victory was forfeited due to treachery and division in the Celtic ranks.

Rivalry between Deira and Bernicia would be a long-running feature of Anglo-Saxon history in the north. In 588, Ethelric of Bernicia slew Aelle. In 603, at Degastan, Ethelric's son Ethelfrith went on to defeat Aidan MacGabrain, king of Dalriada (Argyll, a colony of the Christian Irish Scots), whom St Columba had anointed king in the name of Christ. With his power assured, Ethefrith formalised Bernician rule over both Deira and Bernicia, uniting all the Angle territory north of the River Humber into one kingdom called Northumbria.

Deira was reduced to a mere sub-kingdom. Although Ethelfrith took the slain Aelle's daughter Acha as his wife in order to gain a shred of legitimacy (he later killed her), in Saxon law the male heirs of a slain king retained the right to the throne for two generations. For this reason, Ethelfrith, who did not mind the women remaining in Deira, regarded the young male princes as future threats. The two primary threats were Hilda's uncle Edwin and, as he grew to manhood, her father, Hereric.

Hereric became aware that Ethelfrith wanted rid of him just as Breguswith fell pregnant with Hilda. He fled to Elmet, one of the few Celtic sub-kingdoms that remained in eastern Britain, near today's Leeds. Scholars wonder whether they had friends or relatives there.

Recent DNA research shows that British women have a higher percentage of 'aboriginal' (that is, pre-Saxon) genes than do men. That is not surprising, since the Saxon incomers were males and many of them would have married indigenous Celtic women. There is evidence of Anglo-Saxon kings having Celtic ancestors.[3] This raises a question about Hilda's maternal line. It is likely that her maternal ancestry included some Celtic Britons; some writers assume that her mother, Breguswith, was Celtic, although the name she was given is Saxon.

Elmet's ruler was King Ceretic. Legends identify his father with the poet Gwallog ap Llaennog, one of the Celtic kings who laid siege to the Saxons on the island of Lindisfarne. The Welsh poet Taliesin associates him with Elmet and makes him the stuff of Arthurian legends. Whatever their connections may have been, Hereric was hunted down and poisoned, probably by agents bribed by Ethelfrith—an echo of King Herod, who slew the male infants around Bethlehem upon learning that a male child had been born who some said would become a king.

The distraught Breguswith, left alone in Deira with her child and unborn baby, and not knowing what had happened to her husband, had a dream in her dark night. As she searched diligently but in vain for her husband, she found a most precious necklace under her garment. As she gazed at it attentively, it cast a blaze of light that lit up all of Britain. In recording this story, Bede comments that 'this dream was truly fulfilled in her daughter Hild, whose life was a bright example, not only to herself, but to many who desired to live well' (OUP, p. 313). The fact that Bede thought that the light radiated all of Britain is significant: Hilda's influence would shine among other races, not just among the English.

Reflection

Solveig Flugstad of Norway writes:

My first encounter with Celtic Christianity was the story about the dream that Hilda's mother had when she was pregnant with her. If we believe that the Lord has created us, dreams are an obvious part of his creation and it is strange we do not pay more regard to what happens inside us during the night. People today who are open to this dimension in life live in an unbroken tradition from Old Testament times. Dreams are part of God's care and counselling for us, also![4]

The Bible tells stories of people, who were neither Jews nor Christians, to whom God spoke in dreams. Abraham lived before the Bible was written but God spoke to him in visions (Genesis 15:1). God, who had promised Abraham that his descendants would be more numerous than the stars, even though his ageing wife Sarah was barren, said to him, 'As for Sarai your wife, you shall not call her Sarai, but Sarah [meaning Princess] shall be her name. I will bless her, and moreover I will give you a son by her... and she shall give rise to nations' (Genesis 17:15–16).

A friend wrote the following to me:

My father died just a few days after my conception. My mother never really recovered from this terrible loss... Upon discovering that she was pregnant she returned to her family up north, a relationship fraught with conflict, and there I grew up, loved but torn between adults with conflicting emotional agendas, longing to be looked after but locked into my role as caretaker for a parent locked in grief... I was haunted by the feeling that if I hadn't been conceived when I was, my mother would have stayed in the area, remarried, and been happy. I felt that it was all my fault. This caused problems between myself and my own daughter. I have never felt able to give my little girl the closeness and unforced attention she needs. Then... I found myself reading about Hilda.

Hilda, like myself, was a fatherless child. Her mother Breguswith was comforted by a dream which was a prophecy concerning the future of her daughter. Upon reading these words I saw my conception and prenatal development in a completely different light. Rather than imagining myself as the blight upon my mother's future happiness, I pictured the hands of a loving God surrounding me, literally holding me in my mother's womb and bringing me to birth against remarkable odds. My mother was 39 and in poor health when I was born...

I turned to the liturgy for Hilda[5] and read this verse in Isaiah: 'You will be called Hephzebah (I delight in you).' I was lost in silent prayer and praise. I sensed that just as Jesus said to his disciple John, 'Behold, your mother', so God was now offering me a mother in heaven, no less a person than Hilda herself, who knew my inner pain and was ready with all her wisdom, compassion, diplomacy and grace to guide me and intercede for me.

Even those who do not believe that we should talk to 'saints' will recognise that something deeply healing was being wrought by God in my friend.

Even though Ethelfrith had commandeered Deira's royal quarters at York, Deira's people remained sympathetic to their ousted royal family. Perhaps a friendly landowner offered Breguswith a property where she could bring up Hereswith and Hilda. It is even possible that Ethelfrith's wife Acha, who was Hilda's great-aunt, found them some modest quarters.

The first potential rival whom Ethelfrith sought to eliminate was Edwin, who had been born to King Aelle not long before his death, and was still only a boy. Ethelfrith determined to hunt him down, but God began to work on Hilda's uncle while he took refuge in hard places. Bede tells of the fatherless child-prince 'wandering so many years through all the kingdoms of Britain'. Edwin's experiences must have shaped Hilda, as, in later years, she perhaps listened spellbound to stories of her uncle's exile.

According to Reginald of Durham, Edwin's childhood was spent in what is now Wales. He was fostered among the Celtic Britons in the court of King Cadfan of Gwynedd, where some held the Christian faith. There Edwin met Cadfan's son Cadwallon, who would later become his deadly foe, perhaps because of a boyhood jealousy between son and foster-son. So Ethelfrith declared war on Gwynedd, and then on the neighbouring kingdom of Powys, after Edwin had fled there. By now a young warrior, Edwin went east into Mercia. There he married Coenburg, the daughter of Mercia's King Cearl. They bore two sons, Osfrith and Eadfrith.

The ears of the infant Hilda must have been filled with news of one horror after another, but her ears would also have been filled with news of her relatives' visions of a new God.

Edwin then travelled on to the court of the most powerful English king, the half-evangelised Redwald of the East Angles, and begged his protection. Redwald welcomed Edwin. When this reached the ears of Ethelfrith, he sent messengers who offered Redwald a large bribe if he would hand Edwin over. Redwald refused two such bribes but succumbed to a third, no doubt cowed by Ethelfrith's threat of war. A confidante of Edwin informed him of this and offered to aid his escape in the night. Edwin replied, 'I made an agreement with this great king and I cannot be the first to break it when he has done me no harm and has as yet showed no enmity towards me.'

Edwin left his bedroom and stayed outside, alone. As he sat on a large stone, he was alarmed to see an unfamiliar man approaching him. Edwin, whose hoped-for crown seemed now to elude him, looked at this fair young man, who wore a crown—but it was a crown of thorns in the shape of a cross. The man greeted him and asked why he sat alone and distraught while others were at rest. Edwin asked what business it was of his. The stranger replied, 'Do not think I am ignorant of your plight. I know who you are, why you are here, and what evils you fear. But tell me what reward you would give to someone, if there be such a person, who would release you from your anguish and persuade Redwald neither to harm you nor deliver you to your enemies.' Edwin replied that he would give such a person everything in his power to give. The stranger went on, 'And what if he would promise, with power to effect the promise, that your enemies will be destroyed, that you will be king and surpass in power all who preceded you as kings among the English people?' Edwin, feeling encouraged, promised to show fulsome gratitude to such a benefactor. The stranger asked Edwin a third question: 'If this person who can predict and deliver your future can also give you advice for your salvation and way of life, advice that is better than any of your kinsfolk could give you, will you obey him and accept his counsel?' Edwin promised to follow in every way the counsel of such a person.

The stranger placed his right hand on Edwin's head and declared, 'You must obey the one who first appears to you in this form and in this sign. He will teach you to obey the one living and true God who created all things, the God who will give you what I promise, and who will show you through that man all that you must do. When you encounter this sign, remember this encounter and fulfil your promise without delay.' He suddenly vanished. Edwin realised that his visitor was not from this mortal world.

Edwin stayed seated on the stone, feeling greatly heartened, wondering about the identity of his visitor, when his confidante returned, full of cheer, and told him, 'Go inside and put your fears to rest. The king has changed his mind: he has no plan to harm you and, in fact, is determined to keep faith with you. When he disclosed to the queen his plan to hand you over, she talked him out of it and said it was unworthy of so great a king to betray his best friend in his hour of need for love of money.' Soon after this, Redwald raised a great army and defeated Ethelfrith in a battle on the border of Mercia. Edwin then replaced Ethelfrith as king of Bernicia.

Accounts of this story would circulate through the future monasteries and be reported by Bede, but the longer, earlier account in a *Life of Gregory*, written at Whitby shortly after Hilda's death there, probably owes something to Hilda herself. Two separate episodes seem to have become conflated.

Edwin's original vision of a young, fair man with a cross as his crown was surely a vision of Christ. The man Christ refers to, who would carry the sign of the cross and whose advice Edwin should heed, is Bishop Paulinus, who was neither young nor fair. It is feasible that Paulinus may have visited Redwald's court while Edwin was there, and it is certain that he visited him later.

Bede used this story to buttress his thesis that a king and his kingdom flourished in direct proportion to his adherence to Christian teachings.

Reflection

Some of us are born into a hard place; all of us at times find ourselves in a hard place, surrounded by hard people or circumstances. Hilda's story gives us hope that nothing is too hard for God.

The Bible tells stories of fierce, hardened rulers who were not believers, yet God spoke to them through visions. Nebuchadnezzar, king of the Babylonian empire six centuries before Christ, was so troubled by his dreams that sleep deserted him. When none of his sorcerers could interpret these dreams, the godly Jewish exile Daniel got a message to him and was invited to interpret his dreams. After spending much time in prayer, Daniel explained to the king the meaning of his dream: in years to come, his kingdom would come to an end, and the 'God of heaven' would establish a kingdom that would last for ever. Nebuchadnezzar told Daniel, 'Truly, your God is God of gods and Lord of kings and a revealer of mysteries' (Daniel 2:47) and he promoted Daniel.

In our story we have three royal pagan women, battered and bowed in a fractious kingdom ruled by a hostile usurper. A pattern is emerging in this extraordinary family: God speaks to them through visions. Edwin shows not only a warrior's courage, and skill in making relationships, but also receptivity to visions from a higher power. Breguswith, instead of 'closing down' her life, allows God to speak to her in the vision of the jewels, even though she does not yet know Christ.

God comes in every voice, behind every face, in every memory, deep in every struggle. To close off any of them is to close off the possibility of becoming new again ourselves.
JOAN CHITTISTER[6]

Be thou my vision, O Lord of my heart,
Naught be all else to me save that thou art;
Thou my best thought in the day or the night,
Waking or sleeping, thy presence my light.

High King of heaven, when battle is done,
Grant heaven's joy to me, bright heaven's sun;
Christ of my own heart, whatever befall,
Still be my vision, O Ruler of all.

EIGHTH-CENTURY IRISH, TRANS. MARY BYRNE AND ELEANOR HULL

God, when we are in a hard place,
remind us that you can break through
our brittle shells, our false conditioning
and group mindsets that have no place for you.
You reveal yourself through visions and visitors;
you come in dreams and intimations of the heart;
and we will respond.

In 616, Edwin reconquered Deira and invited his extended family to move into his headquarters at York, where he had been born. Edwin became the most significant male in Hilda's girlhood. This change of fortune was made possible when Redwald slew Ethelfrith on a Mercian battlefield and gave Edwin military assistance in his securing of Deira.

A place, like a person, can have a spirituality, and York had time-honoured roots. It was founded by the Romans in 71 as a fortress of its Ninth Legion, and was called Eboracum. The Romans evidently recognised that the site was strategically located to control the principal south–north route through the Vale of York. It was also well placed to connect with the inland waterway system that later developed; the Ouse was part of this system, and connected to the North Sea via the Humber. The fortress, situated in the north-western section of the future medieval York, attracted a civilian population that settled on the opposite bank of the Ouse, and York became one of the provincial capitals.

In 314, its bishop was summoned to the Council of Arles, along with the bishops of London and another diocese, perhaps Caerleon. The Emperor Constantius had died in York and, in 306, his son Constantine, who later became a Christian, had been declared Emperor there. After the Christianisation of the empire, York became Britain's second most important bishopric.

What happened to York after the departure of the Romans is hazy. Little evidence of the Anglo-Saxon newcomers, or of church buildings before Edwin's time. has yet been found in York by archaeologists. Tradition has it that the great Celtic saint Samson was installed there by 'King' Arthur's uncle, Ambrosius Aurelianus, after he repelled a force of Saxon invaders in AD466. Samson is recognised as York's 'archbishop' by Orthodox churches and is commemorated by present York place names such as St Sampson's Square. We know about Samson from an early *Life*.[7] After education at St Illtyd's great community, at today's Llwantwit Major, he became the abbot of its daughter monastery on Caldey island. Samson modelled an ascetic spirituality. He became a missionary statesman, travelling to Ireland to study, across Cornwall to evangelise, and to Guernsey, where he gave children little treats before telling them Bible stories. Finally he became one of the seven founders of Christian Brittany. It is possible that tradition granted him the status of Archbishop of York because he was pre-eminent among British bishops and made a visitation to York.

The Saxons would have known nothing of Samson, but perhaps the locals passed down stories that the perceptive young Hilda picked up, such as the story of his healing a student brother at St Illtyd's monastery, when everyone else was preparing for the student's funeral.

The Roman roads probably helped to keep York a settlement of some importance as the remnants of the Christian Romano-British society disintegrated. This is supported by the fact that Pope Gregory wrote the following to Augustine of Canterbury in 601:

We wish you also to send a bishop of your own choice to the city of York, and if that city with the adjoining territory accepts the word of God, this bishop is to consecrate twelve other bishops and hold the dignity of Metropolitan. If we live to see this, we intend to grant him the pallium, but he is to remain subject to your authority. After your death, however, he is to preside over the bishops whom he has consecrated and to be wholly independent of the Bishop in London. Thenceforward, seniority of consecration is to determine whether the Bishop of London or of York takes precedence, but they are to consult one another and take united action.[8]

York would remain one of England's most important cities for the next 1300 years. It is still one of only two British cities surrounded by Roman walls (the other is Chester) and is the second of the Church of England's two provinces.

Reflection

Jesus speaks to towns and cities. He spoke to Chorazin, a small town in Galilee: 'Woe to you, Chorazin! ... For if the deeds of power done in you had been done in Tyre and Sidon, they would have repented long ago' (Luke 10:13).

York did welcome messengers of Christ, however, and its leading family, Hilda among them, would respond to the message.

York Minster has an online prayer box: www.yorkminster.org/worship-and-choir/prayer-box.html. I sent this prayer:

May York be a place of
holy learning and hospitality,
divine purpose and prayer,
where the strong serve the weak,
believers listen to the cries of the poor
and share good news with the world.
May her people become one with Hilda and all the saints above.

In whatever place we live, we may ask Christ, 'May your cross free it; may your gentleness woo it; may your peace still it; may your life fill it.'

Between the years 616 and 627, Edwin had a series of experiences that culminated in the baptism of himself and a host of his subjects, including Hilda.

Hilda was perceptive. Did she ponder these experiences and discern a pattern before she decided to take the plunge?

They were tumultuous years of aggression mixed with respect for the power of a higher order that Christianity seemed to bring. Political expansion and victory in battle were necessary parts of being an Anglo-Saxon king. The legal claimants to the Bernician throne were Ethelfrith's young sons Eanfrith and Oswald, who had fled from Northumbria for safety. Edwin, having seized the Bernician capital, was now in charge of the entire Northumbrian kingdom.

Much of Edwin's early military activity concentrated on the southern borders of Northumbria. Around 626, he evicted King Ceretic from Elmet and then captured the Celtic kingdom of Meicen (Hatfield) near Doncaster and the Anglian kingdom of Lindsey (Lincolnshire). On the death of Redwald, Edwin was able to pursue a grand plan to expand Northumbria to pre-eminence among the English kingdoms. He built up a navy. Some time during those years, he declared war on Mon (Anglesey) and the Isle of Man. He followed the way of a Saxon warlord. As Hilda grew up, she would have heard little but reports of battles from her male peer.

The king travelled throughout his land, dispensing justice and collecting rents from his estates, visiting each royal villa once or twice a year. Hilda's family may have joined him on his prolonged stay at Bernicia's royal residence at Yeavering. Between 1952 and 1962, the excavator Brian Hope-Taylor rediscovered the long-lost ruins of buildings there, many associated with King Edwin. In discussing the possible uses of the Great Hall, he drew on the story of Beowulf, in which the royal hall is a place of feasting and drinking, and considered the possibility that platforms along the sides of the hall were used to carry tables and benches, beside which revellers would be rolling in the aisles, convivial horns would be refilled and minstrels would play from table to table. These arrangements were also suitable for ceremonies and processions. Beyond the hall was what he thought to be a large cattle corral, which could have been used to round up cattle or horses brought in as taxes from local people. These animals would inevitably be the source of food for the feasting that took place in the Great Hall during Edwin's stay.[9]

Edwin's worldly power exceeded that of any of his predecessors —but what of that non-worldly power, which had so strangely visited him at Redwald's court? In 626, Edwin asked Kent's Christian princess Ethelburga to become his second wife, his first wife presumably having left him or died. This was partly a political marriage: Edwin wanted Kent as his ally. Ethelburga agreed, on three conditions: that she could practise her Christian faith, that she could bring a Roman priest who would teach the faith to Edwin's subjects, and that Edwin himself would consider becoming a Christian. Edwin agreed to all three conditions, so Ethelburga brought with her the Italian priest Paulinus, who had arrived in England by 604 with the second missionary group from Rome. Bede reports that Paulinus, who was made a bishop before or after his arrival, wished to convert the Northumbrians as well as provide religious services to the new queen. Bede describes him as 'a man tall of stature, a little stooping, with black hair and a thin face, a hooked and thin nose, his aspect both venerable and awe-inspiring'. The man referred to in Edwin's prophetic vision at Redwald's court had arrived. That dream had surely prepared Edwin to be receptive towards his wife's missionary bishop.

Paulinus typically stayed in a royal centre, taught the locals (who were summoned to attend) for about a month, and then baptised them in a river. He stayed at Yeavering and baptised thousands in the nearby River Glen. He baptised many at Holy Stone, near Rothbury, whose large well is still preserved. The *Anglo-Saxon Chronicle* states that the River Swale became known as 'England's River Jordan' because Paulinus baptised tens of thousands in its waters at places such as Catterick Bridge. According to Pope Gregory's plan that York would be England's second metropolitan see, Paulinus established his church there, although he also built churches on other royal estates. Hilda may have been his star pupil. His coming certainly gave her access to wider sources of Christian learning.

Edwin's nobles were not opposed to his accepting the new religion. The famous story is told in the Whitby *Life of Gregory*, and retold by Bede, that Edwin gathered his council of elders, which included his pagan high priest, Coifi. Paulinus outlined the gospel message to him, a colleague of Coifi said:

Your Majesty, when we compare the present life of man on earth with that time of which we have no knowledge, it seems to me like the swift flight of a single sparrow through the banqueting-hall where you are sitting at dinner on a winter's day with your thegns and counsellors. In the midst there is a comforting fire to warm the hall; outside the storms of winter rain or snow are raging. This sparrow flies swiftly in through one door of the hall, and out through another. While he is inside, he is safe from the winter storms; but after a moment of comfort, he vanishes from sight into the wintry world from which he came. Even so, man appears on earth for a little while; but of what went before this life or of what follows, we know nothing. Therefore, if this new teaching has brought any more certain knowledge, it seems only right that we should follow it. (Bede, Penguin, p. 129)

Edwin was not yet converted, but he received letters from Pope Boniface V, urging his conversion.

The mission that Pope Gregory had sent with Augustine in 597 had aimed to convert the entire English people to Christianity, but it had struggled to gain appeal much beyond Kent. The coming of Ethelburga and Paulinus to Northumbria opened up a large opportunity, which needed back-up from the wider church. This came in the form of two letters, accompanied by gifts, sent to Edwin by Pope Boniface V from Rome, the capital of the Christian world. Hilda would have learned about these letters. Boniface addresses Edwin as 'the illustrious king of the English', which must have pleased Edwin.

In his first letter, the Pope explains that it is the 'will of the Supreme Deity' (the God who is co-eternal Father, Son and Holy Spirit), who has created all things, to 'place man above all others' and to communicate, as Christ commanded, good news of salvation to all peoples, for their greater benefit, even to the places on the extreme edge of the earth, as Britain was then thought to be. He therefore implores them to renounce idols and be baptised. The letter was accompanied by gifts, such as a shirt with gold ornaments, which, Boniface explained, carried the blessing and protection of Peter, the prince of apostles. He did not need to add that it also brought status.

Boniface sent separate gifts and a letter to Ethelburga. He rejoices to hear how the queen practises her faith, is saddened to learn that her husband is still bound to pagan practices, and asks how there can be a true marriage union if there is a clash between truth and error. He implores her to try to soften Edwin's hard heart, that the unbelieving husband might be saved, and to inform him when such a conversion takes place so that he may have peace of mind and give thanks.

Paulinus (and God!) kept trying. In 626, Paulinus was with Edwin at the royal quarters near the river Derwent (now known as Londesborough), where the queen had come to celebrate Easter and give birth to their first child. Perhaps Hilda and her mother and sister were there, too. The king of the West Saxons, Quichelm, had sent a message with a man named Eumer, whose real intent was to deprive Edwin of his kingdom and his life. Eumer carried a two-edged knife treated with poison, so that if the blade failed to kill the king, the poison would complete its work. As the emissary delivered his master's message, he suddenly leapt up, drew the knife concealed in his clothes and attacked the king. Immediately a devoted thane named Lilla interposed his body to take the thrust of the dagger. Lilla died and the blade glanced the king behind, who became ill but recovered. Eumer was slain by the thanes. That same night, the holy night of Easter for the queen and Paulinus, Ethelburga gave birth, and Edwin gave thanks to his gods. Paulinus thanked Christ for two safe deliveries and told Edwin that the birth was in answer to his prayers. Edwin promised to convert to Christianity and allow his new daughter, Enfleda, to be baptised—if he won a victory over Wessex.

Even then, according to Bede's account, it was only after Paulinus had reminded him of his night-time encounter at Redwald's court that he finally handed over his life to Christ and arranged for a mass baptism of himself and thousands of his subjects. Among these thousands were Edwin's sons born to him in Mercia, the nobility and ordinary people—and Hilda. They were baptised in the little wooden church that he had built at York. Bede makes a point of saying that later Paulinus began to build a grander church of stone, but that Edwin took care to keep the little oratory within the new church. Did Edwin value a private, simple place of prayer?

What did Hilda and the others promise at their baptism? They would have followed the rite used at Rome in the sixth century, which reflected the one drawn up by Bishop Hippolytus in the third century. Hippolytus taught:

When the person being baptised goes down into the water, he who baptises him, putting his hand on him, shall say: 'Do you believe in God, the Father Almighty?' And the person being baptised shall say: 'I believe.' Then holding his hand on his head, he shall baptise him once. And then he shall say: 'Do you believe in Christ Jesus, the Son of God, who was born of the Virgin Mary, and was crucified under Pontius Pilate, and was dead and buried, and rose again the third day, alive from the dead, and ascended into heaven, and sat at the right hand of the Father, and will come to judge the living and the dead?' And when he says: 'I believe,' he is baptized again. And again he shall say: 'Do you believe in the Holy Spirit, in the holy church, and the resurrection of the body?' The person being baptized shall say: 'I believe,' and then he is baptised a third time.[10]

Baptism was preceded by 40 days of instruction. Some bishops taught that during the 40 days the bishop would go through the whole Bible, beginning with Genesis, first relating the literal meaning of each passage and then interpreting its spiritual meaning. After five weeks' teaching, candidates received the Creed, whose content he would explain in the same way. The following elements were involved in the baptism service: renunciation, profession of faith, blessing of the water, threefold immersion, anointing with chrism and signing with the cross.

Celtic sources portray the baptism of Edwin, and the events before and after it, in a different light from Bede. Bede attaches to his story of the sparrow flight an event that, by other accounts, came later. Edwin asked his pagan high priest Coifi who should destroy the shrines of idols. Bede has Coifi saying, 'I will: I worshipped these things in my foolishness, and now that the true God has granted me wisdom, there is no one who could more fittingly set an example to all by destroying them.' Coifi then mounted a horse, girded with sword and spear, and cut down the shrines. The common people thought he was mad but he commanded his staff to do the same. The largest shrine was at the village of Goodmanham, the Village of Seven Wells, in the Yorkshire Wolds. Archaeologists have confirmed that there was an early Germanic settlement here. There is no record of Celtic British or Irish Christians destroying pagan shrines: that was contrary to their indigenous approach. In the years ahead, Hilda would have to evaluate the merits of these different approaches.

Bede fits the stories he heard into his Roman framework, dominated by the church and Bishop Paulinus. Nennius, who probably drew his material for northern affairs from seventh-century sources at Ninian's Whithorn monastery, fits the stories he heard into his Celtic British framework, which sees little of God in the brutal Saxon invaders. Sometimes their accounts diverge. Nennius, who in this instance is probably more accurate, states that although the infant Enfleda was baptised at Easter in Derwent, the mass baptism of Edwin, his adult family and nobles took place at Pentecost in York, not at Easter as Bede states. The *Annales Cambriae* states that Run, son of Urbgen (probably Urien of Rheged near Carlisle), baptised Edwin, whereas Bede has Bishop Paulinus presiding. The divergent portrayals of these writers reveal a deeper, continuing divergence between two ways of incarnating the Christian gospel—the Celtic and the Roman—which marked the whole of Hilda's life.

It may be that Edwin remained grateful for the childhood protection offered him by his British friends and invited representatives such as Prince Urien to take some part in the great baptism. Whether it was at Easter or Pentecost, and whether or not Celtic as well as Roman Christians shared in it, we know that Hilda and her sister were among the thousands who were baptised that day.

Afterwards, other children of Edwin by Queen Ethelburga were baptised—Ethelhun, Etheidrith and Wuscfrea, the first two of whom died shortly after birth and were buried in the church at York. Ifli, the son of Osfrid, was also baptised, and many more nobles. No doubt Hilda was present at these baptisms, perhaps as a godparent.

In 634 Pope Honorius, who had succeeded Boniface, sent a papal pall to Paulinus as 'Metropolitan of York' and another to his namesake, Honorius, 'Metropolitan of Canterbury'. A pall was a shoulder band with pendants, which signified a special authority. With Paulinus' pall came letters to Edwin, saying that his faith was reported throughout the world and exhorting him and his people to persist in the faith and, with careful mind and constant prayers, to read the works of Boniface's predecessor Pope Gregory the Great. His niece probably read these more assiduously than did Edwin.

Bede eulogised Edwin's reign. He had heard reports that, wherever Edwin's reign extended, this proverb became current: 'A woman with her newborn babe might walk throughout the island, from sea to sea, without receiving any harm.' In several places on highways Edwin caused stakes to be fixed next to springs, with brass dishes hanging at them, for the convenience of travellers; 'nor durst any man touch them for any other purpose than that for which they were designed, either through the dread they had of the king, or for the affection which they bore him.' Bede continues:

His dignity was so great throughout his dominions, that his banners were not only borne before him in battle, but even in time of peace, when he rode about his cities, towns, or provinces, with his officers, the standard-bearer was wont to go before him. Also, when he walked along the streets, that sort of banner which the Romans call Tufa, and the English, Tuuf, was in like manner borne before him.

The cult of kingship became Christianised and would have influenced Hilda. More than a century later, in 793, Alcuin, writing home to Northumbria from the court of the Holy Roman Emperor Charlemagne, declared, 'In the righteousness of the king is the prosperity of the whole people, the victory of the war-host, the mildness of the seasons, the fruitfulness of land.'[11]

Who were Hilda's role models during her childhood and adolescence? Her mother, sister and aunt surely ranked among the females. Breguswith, that tough pagan woman with a seer's eye—did she become a Christian with Edwin? The fact that both her daughters consecrated themselves so completely to Christ might suggest that she did. Hilda's sister Hereswith married Ethelric, a committed Christian who became heir to the East Anglian throne.

The most dominant male role model in Hilda's early years was surely Edwin, a man of courage and flair in surviving, in waging battles and in giving loyalty to allies, who was not so wrapped up in himself that he could not take seriously visions from within and new ideas from abroad. The traumatic family saga of Hilda's childhood must have affected her profoundly, and surely she inherited and imbibed some of her uncle's characteristics. He had the wisdom to consult with his shrewdest advisers and he often sat alone, in silence, for long periods, deliberating in his heart how he should proceed and which religion to adopt. We do not know if Edwin took upon himself to be something of a surrogate father to Hilda: it would seem to be in character if he did. What we do not know is the dark side that Hilda may also have seen in him, and whether other men modelled for her a different face of Christ.

Nor do we know how Hilda related to her great-aunt Ethelburga, but we can be sure that Hilda would have been included in her aunt's desire that her chaplain and Christian staff should teach them the Christian faith. The adult Hilda was very well educated, so she no doubt took every opportunity to learn from royal tutors from an early stage. Was it then that Hilda began to learn Latin, the language they used for the Bible and the prayers, and to meditate daily on the scriptures?

Did Hilda follow her sister into marriage? She took no monastic vows of celibacy at the time of her baptism, and it was almost inevitable that a princess not in vows would marry. None of the early accounts refer to her as a virgin. If she married one of Edwin's nobles, her husband may have been slain in battle with Edwin. Christine Fell asks why Bede is so curiously blank about the first 33 years of Hilda's life but then writes a flurry of words about Hilda at the age of 33, when she sought to become a nun. One explanation would be that she became a widow at that time. Possibly she had been married to a pagan, which would have made all the more poignant Bede's comment that during her first 33 years she preserved her faith 'inviolate'.[12]

So much classic spirituality has been subverted by the idea that saints have to be virgins and that sex and family life are somehow second-rate. The fact that Bede, who calls every woman he wishes to extol a 'virgin', makes an exception for Hilda and describes her as a 'servant of God', makes me think that Hilda did marry. Certainly Hilda did not collude with the heresy that virginity was innately superior. She stands for a spirituality of wholesomeness in marriage, in work and in all of life.

How precarious was the seat of even the most powerful of earthly kings! The growing strength of Edwin's Northumbria forced the Anglo-Saxon Mercians, under Penda, into an alliance with the Welsh King Cadwallon of Gwynedd, and together they invaded Edwin's lands. They slew him at the Battle of Hatfield Chase in 633.

Many of the people who had professed baptism returned to their pagan gods: their faith was skin-deep. Hilda, however, did not. It seems that Christ himself, the King of kings, had attracted her and drawn her allegiance for life. The waters of baptism had flooded her heart and head, not just her body. Bede stresses her achievement in keeping the faith: she would keep the faith during years of pain and exile, and perhaps even while married to a pagan.

Reflection

This entire first chapter is about a hard, pagan people and its princess, whose traumatic birth and girlhood meant that she lived in a hard place. It is also about how, despite this, God spoke to the people around her in visions. The New Testament as well as the Old reminds us that God works in such ways. Acts 10 tells how a pagan (a Gentile) received a vision and how Peter (a Jewish Christian) received a separate but linked vision. This revealed to him that God could speak to anyone in the world who seeks to do what is right. It brought him into touch with the pagan, who was named Cornelius. This kind of thing still happens.

A man phoned me, saying, 'I am not a Christian; I have never read the Bible. I've had a dream, then I read your book.[13] Can I come to the retreat you are leading in Glastonbury?' Glastonbury, in England, is the Avalon of Arthurian myth. There, pagan, earth, esoteric and religious spiritualities flow and ebb. In his dream, the man saw a pure white hand descend from above and touch his heart. His heart melted. Upon waking, he shook and sobbed for three days. He asked a vicar what it meant, and was told that it was the Holy Spirit. At the retreat, this man read the Bible for the first time, aloud, and he turned to Christ.

Pagans, Muslims and many others are having dreams about Jesus. What significant dream do you know about? If you don't know about any, why not ask people about their dreams? Why not have a pen and paper by your bed so that, if you wake after a dream, you can write it down and reflect upon what it might be telling you?

Also reflect on the fact that before Edwin accepted the new faith, he called a council of his elders and asked them what they thought. He tried to build a consensus and to take people with him. What may you learn from his example about team building?

Spirituality of exile:
faith among the East Anglians

When Hilda heard in 633 that Edwin had been slain (and perhaps, if she was married, her husband along with him), she would have fled. Her most likely refuge would have been her sister's extended royal family in East Anglia. Although this family was Christian and loving, Hilda was an exile, mourning the loss of her homeland. We can only guess what agonies engulfed her as one piece after another of dark, disturbing news trickled through—that Cadwallon was wreaking havoc upon Northumbria as he sought to capture it; that Ethelfrith's exiled son Eanfrith had tried to seize Bernicia, and that Osric, a nephew of Edwin's father, had returned to Deira; that Eanfrith had renounced his Christian faith in order to attract the support of Northumbria's war-lusting warriors as they so lightly cast aside their Christian professions and invoked their ancient gods; that cruelties had torn her beloved homeland to shreds and soaked it in blood. What further fears plagued her when she heard that both Osric and Eanfrith had been killed, leaving a power vacuum yet again?

A spirituality of exile weaves its way in and out of the Bible. Israel's religion was forged in the hard desert experiences of Moses' exiles from Egypt. Despite repeated appeals to heed the lessons of that exile, their heirs strayed from God and experienced exile again in the Babylonian empire. Psalmists sang songs of exile: 'How could we sing the Lord's song in a foreign land?' (Psalm 137:4). Jesus' entire life can be viewed as one long exile from his rightful home: 'He came to his own home, and his own people did not accept him' (John 1:11).

A Welsh priest, Andrew Jones, has pictured today's churchgoers as in a kind of exile.[14] They are in exile from the familiar landmarks of Christendom, which, after more than a millennium, are gone. The response God calls for, he suggests, is for Christians to live their lives as a perpetual pilgrimage. There is value as well as sadness in exile. Exile strips us of our dependency upon familiar things that can become a substitute for God. Exile can lead us to embrace God in the here and now, wherever we are, whatever our circumstances. Exile can spur us to redeem the time. The greatness of God-guided personalities is often forged in exile.

What may we learn from Hilda's exile? God had been at work in the land of her exile and in its neighbours. South of Northumbria was the client state of Lindsey (Lincolnshire). The kingdom of the East Angles (Norfolk and Suffolk) was south of Lindsey. Edwin, grateful for the support he once received from East Anglia's King Redwald, had undertaken to convert East Anglia with Paulinus. Sigeberht, the devout half-brother of Hilda's brother-in-law Ethelric, became king. He longed to become a monk (and eventually did), so he invited Ethelric to rule jointly with him.

East Anglia is flat and offers wide horizons, unlike Deira, where hill-surrounded settlements can shut themselves off from new influences. We imagine that Hilda took a keen interest in her brother-in-law's initiatives to build up the church and welcome Christian leaders from other places. Hereswith and Ethelric had a son named Eadwulf. Perhaps Hilda was present at the birth, and most surely she would have met royal neighbours at his baptism.

Ethelric and Sigeberht established Felix, from the Frankish kingdom of Burgundy, as the first bishop of the Eastern Angles at

Dommoc (Dunwich) or Felixstowe. Following the establishment of communities of prayer, learning and hospitality by the Irish monk Columbanus, where Felix may have trained, a wave of enthusiasm led Frankish nobles to establish more such communities for both women and men. Canterbury's Archbishop Honorius had used Felix to evangelise in Kent, and now, as bishop, Felix established East Anglia's first school. Hilda in exile learned about the inspired Christianity of Frankia (France) and Felix.

Shortly after Felix's arrival in East Anglia, the prophetic wandering monk Fursey arrived from Ireland with his brothers Foillan and Ultan and other disciples. Fursey had gone from Frankia to Ireland, where he had drawn great crowds to hear the good news of Christ. Because his spirituality was the opposite of a personality cult, he and his brothers decided to get on a boat and let God's wind blow them to a foreign land in greater need of their message. When God's wind blew them to East Anglia, they called on King Sigeberht, who gave them land for a monastic community at Cnobheresburg (Burgh Castle), near today's Great Yarmouth in Norfolk, where there was an abandoned Roman fort. There they built a kind of village of God from which they tirelessly ventured out to bring their message to the East Angles.

In a vision during illness, Fursey saw four fires—Falsehood, Covetousness, Discord and Cruelty—that threatened to destroy the world. Ever afterwards he pointed out to each person he met, with an intensity that made him sweat, that they had to choose between what destroys and what brings indestructible life. The record of these visions (now lost) began a genre that reached its flower in Dante's *Paradise Lost* and *Paradise Regained*. On another occasion, Fursey heard the words, 'The saints shall advance from one virtue to another: the God of gods shall be seen among us' (see Psalm 84:7). He lived in the light of that vision. Stories of Fursey would surely have reached the ears of Hilda and the royal family, and perhaps stirred their blood. Just as Hilda's childhood had been influenced by stories about Roman role models, so her adulthood was beginning to be influenced, even in East Anglia, by stories of Irish role models.

We cannot be sure of the exact dates when Hilda was in East Anglia, nor of the various reigns of East Anglian kings, but, whether near or afar, she mourned a succession of royals. Following the deaths of Sigeberht and Ethelric in 636, and three devout uncles who all had short reigns, Hilda's nephew Eadwulf took the throne.[15]

Where might the exiled Hilda have lived? In 1939, archeologists unearthed two sixth- and early seventh-century cemeteries at Sutton Hoo, near Woodbridge in Suffolk, and a ship with a wealth of Anglo-Saxon artefacts. Subsequent archaeological campaigns explored the wider site, which now has a visitor's centre. It is thought likely that the ship was King Redwald's burial tomb. Nearby, at Rendlesham, the palace of the East Anglian kings of that period was discovered. Peter Warner, author of *The Origins of Suffolk*, has shown that this whole area may have been part of a single seventh-century royal estate, now subdivided between the parishes of Rendlesham, Bromeswell, and Eyke. So Hilda may have lived there.[16]

There were also other royal quarters. According to the *Liber Eliensis*,[17] Exning near Newmarket, some ten miles from Ely Cathedral, was the place where a royal daughter was born in 631. If Exning was the residence of Hereswith, Hilda may have been present at the birth of King Anna's daughter Ethelthryth. This niece of Hereswith is known to us as St Etheldreda or St Audrey.[18] Etheldreda was married at an early age (twelve was normal) to Tondberht of today's southern Fens, but she remained a virgin. On his death, around 655, she retired to the Isle of Ely, her dowry. In 660, for political reasons, she was married to Northumbria's 15-year-old prince Egfrith. He agreed that she should remain a virgin, as in her previous marriage, but twelve years later he pressed that their marital relationship be consummated. Etheldreda, advised by Northumbria's Bishop Wilfred, refused, despite Egfrith's bribes. She became a nun at

Coldingham under her aunt Ebbe in 672 and founded a double monastery at Ely in 673.

We should not imagine that Hilda in exile was withdrawn or complaining. It is not improbable that Hilda taught the infant Etheldreda prayers and proverbs and lullabies, and it would be entirely in keeping with the character of both women that Hilda later became something of a soul friend to her.

In Frankia, a number of double monasteries for men and women, under a single abbess, had been founded—earlier than any in England—with the monastic boom that followed the missionary activity of Columbanus around 600. Columbanus himself founded several male monasteries in Gaul and, later, in Bobbio in Italy, but the double monasteries of northern Frankia seem to have been conceived as a result of rather than by his mission. Three of the most notable, established with the help of donations from aristocratic women, were Faremoutiers, Jouarre and Chelles. We know from Bede that in the mid-seventh century, English women of high rank went to the double monasteries in northern Frankia, especially to Chelles, because England had none. Hereswith and probably Hilda visited them and made friendships.

An important factor was the legal position of women. Under both Frankish and Anglo-Saxon law, they could receive, own and bestow property. Burgundofara, the founding abbess of Fare-moutiers, had been inspired by Columbanus as a young girl, and her family founded the monastery for her. She was able to leave a will that secured property for the monastery after her death. Once in existence, the double monasteries began to fill a number of social as well as religious needs, and their abbesses and nuns acquired an education and training similar to that of monks.

Chelles had been established by Bathild, its first abbess. Bathild was related to East Anglia's last pagan king, whom Sigeberht ousted after having spent some time in the Frankish court. Bathild was sold into slavery as a young girl and served in the household of King Clovis II's mayor. Clovis and his household became Christians; so did Bathild, and Clovis chose her as his queen. Bathild was quite some woman. Later, when her husband died (between 655 and 658) and she served as queen regent, she sought the freedom of child slaves and abolished the practice of trading Christian slaves. She gave generously to charities until her son came of age in 664 and she was forced into a convent.

Hilda, like her sister, was inspired by what she heard. Like her sister, she may have become a friend of Bathild.

Reflection

When Hilda fled into exile, she was fortunate to have her sister's family to welcome her; even so, she lived with holes in her heart. So many people in our world have been forced to flee their homelands after civil war. They feel displaced and cover their pain by clothing themselves in nostalgic stories, but they do not live in the present. Some exiles in Britain today—exiles in a different but no less profound way—sell *The Big Issue* on the streets. Others are helped by relatives with greater income, but they may feel humiliated because they do not know how to receive. They may not know that all things ultimately come from God and that, therefore, we are brothers and sisters, children of God: the earth and God are our common home.

The writer Aleksandar Hemon left Sarajevo in 1992, just before war hit his home city, and emigrated to the USA. In his autobiography *The Book of My Lives* he writes, 'The decaying elephant in our room was the loss of our previous life.' He used writing as a means of retreat into his interior life but then discovered that 'love is a process of finding a common vision of reality'.[19]

Many of us at some point have to leave our homes because of work or family requirements, or loss of income, loved ones or health, or because our housing subsidy is withdrawn when we lose a family member. We can become morose, a prisoner of our past. We have yet to discover that exile is not the end of everything.

The possibility that we can embrace a spirituality of exile is a lifeline. We acknowledge that every human being's sojourn on this earth is temporary, that we depend upon others for our birth and dying and are called at all times to embrace our vulnerability. We regard our lives not as our possession but as a journey with God in which we give and receive from fellow-travellers.

Exile is not only about the pain of losing what is familiar; it is also an opportunity to learn from new faces and so to broaden and deepen our lives. The prophet Jeremiah urged Jewish exiles in Babylon to work for the good of their cities (Jeremiah 29:7). Hilda seems to have taken that approach. The East Angles among whom she now lived had become Christians largely through the Roman missionaries from Kent, and had adopted their customs. Yet, because they had truly Christian hearts, they were open to Christian influences wherever they came from: they were neither legalistic nor pedantic. In exile Hilda embraced this spirituality. It was because the East Anglian Christians could see Christ in the face of a stranger that they welcomed Fursey, the prophetic monk from Ireland, and it is why Hilda and her sister developed fellowship with women's monasteries in Frankia that were inspired by the Irish tradition of Columbanus.

Columbanus preached that our life is a road:

Home is not a place, it's a road to be travelled, we say,
Our only defence is the armour of God,
With the Gospel of Peace our feet are shod;
So alone, alone,
We walk into the great unknown.[20]

Hilda would probably have learned about Columbanus and the Irish *peregrini*, who went into exile from home and became perpetual pilgrims. She may have learned about the red, white and blue martyrs (that is, witnesses to Christ) that the Irish spoke so much about. The red martyrs were those who had been killed under earlier persecutions of Christians in the Roman Empire, rather than deny Christ. White martyrs were the *peregrini*, such as Columbanus, Fursey and Felix, who in most cases never returned to their birthplaces. Blue martyrs (blue being the colour of death) were those who, although they stayed in their own land, put to death earthly attachments and dedicated themselves to God in long vigils. Such people could navigate exile: such was Hilda.

How may we live life as a pilgrimage? We might start by reflecting on the following poem:

Some people travel in straight lines:
Sat in metal boxes, eyes ahead,
Always mindful of their target,
moving in obedience to coloured lights and white lines,
mission accomplished at journey's end.

Some people travel around in circles:
Trudging in drudgery, eyes looking down,
Knowing only too well their daily, unchanging round,
Moving in response to clock and to habit,
Journey never finished yet never begun.

I want to travel in patterns of God's making:
Walking in wonder, gazing all around,
Knowing my destiny, though not my destination,
Moving to the rhythm of the surging of his Spirit,
A journey which, when life ends, in Christ has just begun.[21]

Lord, if we pine for loved childhood landscapes now for ever gone
Journey with us, You who had nowhere to lay your head.
Lord, if we are distressed at losing the furniture of our lives
Journey with us, You who had nowhere to lay your head.
If we have lost loved ones or limbs, homes or hopes,
Journey with us, You who had nowhere to lay your head.

A spirituality of human warmth:

meeting Aidan of Ireland

We know neither when nor where Hilda first met Aidan, the Irish bishop invited to lead a new mission to Northumbria in 635, but we do know that Hilda was profoundly impressed by Aidan and embraced his spirituality to the end of her life.

When the exiled Hilda learned that, following Eanfrith's blood-bath and speedy death, his younger brother Oswald had crossed into Northumbria with a band of warriors supplied by Dalriada, and had been welcomed as king, she may have felt confused. On the one hand, it was her uncle Edwin who had killed Oswald's father Ethelfrith and usurped his place as king of Northumbria. On the other hand, the boy Oswald had found refuge among the Christian rulers of the Irish Scots and had become a Christian.

The Dalriadans made treaty obligations to the children of Ethelric. Since Oswald was now the exile next in line to Northumbria's throne, they supplied him with warriors. The medieval Scottish historian Fordun, who draws on earlier sources independent of Bede, writes:

The King [of Dalriada] gave them full leave to go away or come back—and even promised them help against Penda or any of the Saxons; but he altogether refused it against Cadwallon and the Britons, who had long been bound to the Scots by the friendship of a faithful alliance. Moreover, though less moved thereto by a liking for the Saxon race than by zeal for the Christian religion, he sent with them a strong body of warriors, to the end that they might safely cross the marches of his kingdom. Being, therefore, supported by so large a host, they entered their father's kingdom, and were gladly welcomed by the inhabitants.[22]

Despite Cadwallon's vast forces, and perhaps because so many Northumbrians joined his cause as he rode south, Oswald won a decisive victory against Cadwallon. The fact that the victors were Christians must have been some solace to Hilda, but she could hardly expect that a member of the family whose members her uncle had slain would welcome back his niece. No doubt she thought it prudent to stay where she was and observe developments.

Almost the first thing Oswald did, once he had secured the Bernician capital, Bamburgh, was to hasten to the kingdom of Lindsey, the buffer state between East Anglia and Northumbria, and, after a short skirmish, secure its allegiance. Hilda doubtless heard about this, and heard also that Oswald went on to make alliances with neighbouring Celtic Christian and Saxon kingdoms; the situation was becoming more stable. Then she heard that Oswald had asked Dalriada's monastery on the Isle of Iona, founded by Columba of Ireland in 563, to send a mission to reconvert his people and her people to Christ, and that, after a failed first mission, a certain Bishop Aidan had arrived.

It is possible that Hilda did not return to Northumbria and meet Aidan until after Oswald's reign, but I think that unlikely. It was in character for Oswald to reach out to neighbouring royals, to be magnanimous, build bridges, encourage reconciliation and mobilise every support possible for the mission to his people. It was therefore likely that he would send a message to the East Anglian court affirming that the exiled women of Deira were welcome to return, and that he would introduce Princess Hilda to

Aidan. I sometimes imagine that Oswald invited her to the Easter festivities at Bamburgh, after which she visited the first monastery and school that Aidan had established at nearby Lindisfarne.

Surely Hilda saw the irony of it all? Her uncle Edwin had become what Bede termed the 'Bretwalder' of the English peoples—the first among its kings. Now Oswald seemed set to become exactly the same. Edwin had been a child refugee among a British Celtic people who claimed to be Christians. Oswald had been a child refugee among the Irish Celts in the north who followed Christ's ways. Edwin and Oswald had both regained the throne, and both invited a Christian mission to their people.

Hilda had felt such disappointment when so many of her people whom Paulinus had baptised returned to their pagan gods after Edwin was killed. Something was wrong with their understanding of the faith if they thought that God was a competitor in battlefield success stakes, a being to be bargained with. The followers of Christ whom she read about in the Gospels did not think like that. True, the men ran away when Jesus was crucified, but they returned— and they stayed. Did her people have a second chance? Would they be given a deeper understanding of what it meant to follow Christ?

If she did feel able to return to Northumbria, then, it said a great deal for both Oswald and Hilda, and for the power of the Christian gospel to create fellowship between peoples. What she discovered through her meeting with Aidan and his brothers in mission was a radically different expression of the Christian gospel. The contrasts between Aidan's ways and those of Paulinus were so stark, so striking, that neither she nor her people would ever be the same again.

The first thing to strike her was probably their different life-styles. Paulinus dressed as a dignitary and spent donors' money on church buildings. Aidan dressed in the simple woollen clothes of ordinary people and gave donations to the poor. He even refused to ride a horse, for that would have put him above the poor, who could not afford horses.

A second contrast was their different approaches to mission. Under Edwin, people were commanded to come to the royal centres and listen to one man, Paulinus. Aidan walked with brothers, unescorted, among the people far from the royal centres. As they walked, they memorised and meditated upon the Gospels. Aidan taught his brothers to greet and befriend each person they met, and to listen to their stories and beliefs. Only then did they ask if their new friend would like to hear their own stories and beliefs.

Today we call this 'interfaith dialogue'. The result was that the people began to trust and love these Christian brothers and invite them into their own settlements. There, the Christians could pray for them, teach, befriend and baptise them in a way that enabled them to remain true to themselves. Such was the welcome given to Aidan and the brothers that they had to send for many more missionaries from Iona and Dalriada and perhaps Ireland, too, who all followed the same humble approach. The faith took root at ground level for the first time and spread like wildfire. Bede wrote:

When anyone met such a monk or priest on the road, they ran to him and bowed, eager to be signed by his hand or receive a blessing from his lips. Whenever he spoke he was given an attentive hearing... When a priest visited a village, the people were quick to gather in some cottage to hear the word of life, for priests and clerics always came to a village solely to preach, baptise, visit the sick and, in short, to care for the souls of its people...

[Aidan's] teaching won the hearts of everyone because he taught what he and his followers lived out. He neither sought nor cared for the possessions of this world, and he loved to give away to the poor the gifts he received from the rich.

A third difference that must have struck Hilda was their models of the church. Paulinus thought that the way to spread the gospel was to make the church the most prestigious institution in the world, through its buildings and clergy. Aidan thought that, in addition to telling the message, they had to model the kingdom of God on earth, to establish little communities—'colonies of heaven'—that were like villages of God for people of all backgrounds. These little villages were not prestigious but they combined daily prayer and work, hospitality and learning, meditation, mission and community. Aidan's first monastery, on the tidal island of Lindisfarne, had wooden huts for the monks, workers, guests and students, and a simple wooden church. Bede, with his Roman sympathies, thought that the larger stone church that replaced Aidan's wooden church was more 'befitting of the dignity of a bishop'; Aidan did not think so. Before the end of Hilda's life, scores, perhaps hundreds, of these little monastic faith communities dotted Northumbria's landscape—as well as a few large ones.

If wealthy people, some of whom doubtless wished to twist Aidan's arm, gave him donations, this would not deter him from challenging their unjust treatment of the poor. He would go to the slave market, use the money to buy a slave his freedom, and then perhaps offer him a job at the 'village of God'.

There was a fourth difference between the Roman and Irish styles. The Christianity introduced by Paulinus was an indoor religion. Once they were baptised, people had to come out of the cold into an ornamented building called a church. The Irish Christians, by contrast, left their indoor comforts in order to go outdoors. They loved the stories of the fourth-century desert fathers and mothers of Egypt, who left the second-hand faith of comfortable cities to live alone with God in wilderness places, there to engage in spiritual warfare with the devil. The Irish kept three seasons of Lent, not one, so that they could make vigil in wild places. Hilda doubtless heard that one of Aidan's first acts was to make a retreat on the uninhabited Inner Farne Isle, and that many of those who followed him did likewise. He taught his flock to fast and pray for 40 days on any piece of land that was to have buildings erected on it for a faith community: it was important to engage in spiritual battle in order to cleanse the land of bad influences.

The elements, for the Irish Christians, were expressions of God among which they should make their home. Bede 'tamed' Hilda, filtering out human characteristics that did not conform to his template of ecclesiastical correctness, but his description of her as a 'woman of energy' was perhaps a hint that she loved the boundless and natural forces of God. Surely she strode the moors, loved the land and relished the outdoors approach of the Irish Christians.

A fifth distinctive contribution made by the Irish was the idea of the *anam cara*, or soul friend. 'A person without a soul friend is like a person without a head,' they taught. It is clear that Aidan inculcated this belief. Cuthbert, one of the great Anglo-Saxon bishops trained by Aidan's mission, had a soul friend, and we shall discover how soul friendship became a hallmark of Hilda's own ministry.

A sixth characteristic of Aidan's approach was more intangible. Sooner or later, Hilda would have heard about the first failed mission from Iona, led by a man named Corman, and Aidan's advice at a post-mortem meeting of that monastery's council. His advice, in effect, was to find out what people were hungering for, and give them 'milk'. What an utterly different approach this was, compared to the one that Hilda had known, which emphasised externals—pressing people to leave their own communities and eat the spiritual foreign fare placed before them. Milk comes from within the mother and is absorbed by the child. Aidan was offering something gentle and organic that sustained both weak and strong people. Sooner or later, perhaps Hilda sensed that she herself could offer a spiritual mother's milk.

The differences in approach between the Irish and the Romans were indeed far-reaching, but it was Aidan himself who touched Hilda's heart. His name in Irish meant 'Little flame', and it was his human warmth that endeared him to her above all else. Over time she observed him at the monastery, at the court, and among the poor: he was always the same person. There was nothing false about him. He treated everyone as a child of God, without fear or favour. She came to value the gentleness, the affection, the unaffected spontaneity, the holistic rhythms and the authenticity of the Irish Christians. Bede put it this way:

I have described... his love of peace and charity, temperance and humility; his soul which triumphed over anger and greed, and at the same time despised pride and vainglory... and his tenderness in comforting the weak, in relieving and protecting the poor.

These two Christians, Aidan and Hilda, came from such different backgrounds, yet both had remained true to themselves and to their God: there was a chemistry between them. Hilda would carry in her heart the warmth and the ways of the Irish 'pilgrims for the love of God', as some described them, to the end of her days. But would she and Aidan be ships that passed in the night and then drifted apart for ever? It seemed so, for circumstances again forced Hilda into exile among her East Anglian relatives.

What were these circumstances? There are several possibilities, but I think the most likely was the death of Oswald. The year 642 was a tragic turning point for Aidan's mission. Domnall Brecc, the ruler of Dalriada, was killed in the battle of Strathcarron; and Oswald, Aidan's sponsor, who would be honoured as a model of a Christ-like king throughout Europe for many centuries, was killed in the battle of Maserfield by the pagan tyrant Penda, who horribly dismembered his body. Penda displayed these body parts to discourage anyone from ever again daring to stand up to him. If Hilda had moved back among her Deiran people during Oswald's reign, it was surely upon his death that she returned to East Anglia as an exile again. If she had married a second time, perhaps to one of the Deiran warriors who fought and died with Oswald, she would twice have lost husband and home. Certainly, she returned to East Anglia alone. It may be that she had had enough of the heartbreaks and upheavals of Northumbria, and that she found happiness among the friends, family and faith of the East Anglian royals whose family she had entered through her sister's marriage.

Ethelfrith, whom Edwin had slain, had yet one more son left alive—Oswy, Oswald's younger brother, who was entitled to rule in Bernicia. He was beleaguered at home, for Dalriada was in turmoil and Penda now stood unchallenged as the power in the land of the English. Northumbria reverted to its two sub-kingdoms of Deira and Bernicia.

News came through to Hilda, back in East Anglia, that Oswy had secured Bamburgh and become the ruler of Bernicia. He, like Oswald, had been taught the Christian faith at Iona, and he did not return to the apostasy of Oswald's immediate predecessors. Aidan stayed as bishop. Iona had somehow succeeded where Paulinus' Kentish mission had failed, in holding Northumbria for the faith.

Hilda's homeland, Deira, welcomed to its throne Oswin, the grandson of Aelle's brother Elfric, a devoted Christian and a distant relative of Hilda. Oswin told Aidan that he must remain bishop of all Northumbrians and therefore of the Deirans, and have a bishop's see at York, as well as at Lindisfarne. Aidan began to spend time at York and became familiar with that place of Hilda's baptism, which the Pope had decreed should be the second see of the English church.

During this period, the Deirans lived in constant fear that Penda, who had grabbed the land on their southern border, might invade, and this may be a reason why Hilda did not at first return.

By 643, Oswy was strong enough to secure a Kentish princess as his queen: his first Celtic wife had either died or been left behind. Oswy's queen was none other than Enfleda, the daughter born to Hilda's uncle Edwin and his Kentish wife at Easter, on the night of Edwin's near-assassination, who had returned with her mother to Kent when Edwin was killed. Hilda now had 'family' in Bernicia. It was too dangerous to transport Enfleda by land, but one of Aidan's monks, Utta, Abbot of Gateshead, led a sea escort—though he had to cast oil blessed by Aidan to still the raging waves. Hilda may have felt it was too dangerous to attend the wedding, but, as things improved, she perhaps made visits to Enfleda at Bamburgh and met with Aidan again.

We know beyond doubt that in midlife Hilda decided to become a nun. Her sister Hereswith, once her husband had been slain (or perhaps after an agreed separation), set out to take her vows at the Chelles monastery in Frankia with which they had been forging links. Hilda was prepared to leave behind the traumas and attachments of Northumbria and dedicate the rest of her days to the religious life across the sea. She had an affinity with two women with whom she looked forward to working— her sister Hereswith and Abbess Bathild.

That, however, was not to be the end of her story. Word of her plans reached Aidan and he jumped. As he thought of Hilda living out vows across the sea, he thought also of another tradition, beloved of the Irish, that he had not so far been able to introduce to the English—the spiritual foster mother. The Irish, with their vivid imagination, gleaned from the Gospels that Christ had needed twelve male apostles and as many women to make possible his mission in the small province of Judea. If the same kind of things as happened in the Gospels were to happen in Ireland, it too needed both its apostles and its spiritual foster mothers. Pre-Christian Ireland already had a custom, among the landowners at least, of parents sending their children to be mentored by a foster parent who could supplement the natural parents' provision, steeping the child in their culture and in social skills. As Christianity spread, wise and holy women—hermits, widows, members of monasteries—developed this role further until the spiritual foster mothers became the heart of Christian Ireland.

Aidan had come to the English with only male brothers. He had no choice: Iona was an island and allowed only men. But gradually, I suspect, he came to realise that there were parts of the English people that only women could reach, and that the English needed their spiritual foster mothers as much as did Ireland. Without them, the full nature of God could not be experienced and the English could not be truly birthed in Christ, as distinct from having the externals of religion placed upon them.

Aidan had made a small beginning and had encouraged a few women to take vows. The first woman in Northumbria he consecrated was Heiu, who came from Ireland and was probably a princess. In 640, he placed her in charge of a small group of women and men who wished to live by vows on 'the island of the Hart' (Hartlepool), but Heiu hankered to leave and become a recluse. If the legendary medieval *Life of Saint Bega* is to be believed, King Oswald arranged for the Irish princess to find sanctuary in Northumbria, in which case Aidan must have received her vows. St Bees Head, in Cumbria, is named after the hermitage she is thought to have established there. The Saxon parents of a lad named Cuthbert—converts, we presume, of Aidan's mission—had provided him with a spiritual mother named Kenswith. Cuthbert would become an outstanding leader after Aidan's death. These developments, however, were but drops in the ocean. Any major breakthrough had so far eluded Aidan.

We sometimes know God's will only by becoming aware of something that is its opposite—some area of neglect, perhaps, or a vital part of Christ's universal body that is missing. A frustration or a disappointment may alert us to it. Hearing that something elsewhere is coming to birth may spur us to realise that some such thing was meant to come to birth in our own field of endeavour. Pangs of longing, a sinking feeling in the pit of the stomach that we have missed the boat—any of these can awaken us to a crossroads moment, a moment of synchronicity, a moment of significance for the future. I suspect that Aidan felt such emotions when he heard that Princess Hilda, a born leader, a tried and tested Christian, would be leaving the English people in order to fulfil her monastic vocation abroad.

Aidan's heart may have missed a beat but he did not miss the moment. He sent an urgent message to Hilda. He said, in effect (as Lord Kitchener said centuries later), 'Your country needs you.' 'It needs you to help us pioneer monasteries and learning and fostering of women and men among the English.'

What questions had Hilda asked herself as she reached her crossroads at the age of 33? What was her calling? What did common sense indicate? Where would she feel most comfortable and have access to most resources?

Hilda's natural response might have been, 'But we have to be trained, and there are no monasteries where we can be trained among the English.' Aidan's response was magnificent—and Irish: if there were no training monasteries for women in Northumbria, he and members of his team would train her through frequent visits. Not for him the icy separation between men and women that marked the Roman churches and even the desert fathers. Hilda was the woman who could make his vision a reality, and nothing must get in the way.

We do not know what messages were relayed and what discussions took place, but we know that Hilda came. It indicates a degree of belief in Aidan and what he stood for, so strong that she was willing to set aside protocol, family and security and risk all for the greatest adventure of her life. Paulinus, who died about that time, would have turned in his grave.

Hilda was given a 'hide of land' somewhere on the north side of the River Wear. A hide was an area of land between 60 and 120 acres, sufficient to provide a livelihood for an extended family. There she developed a small band of women who lived a rhythm of prayer and work. Aidan and his colleagues did indeed visit her often. As Bede records, 'Bishop Aidan, and others of the religious that knew her, frequently visited her and loved her heartily, and diligently instructed her.' Although Hilda may have protested that she had no training in the monastic vocation, she had access to the best teachers and books, both at Edwin's court and in East Anglia. She had probably read more widely than Aidan. What she learned from the brothers, however, could not be learned from books. She learned how to live a set of values, an authentic way of life; she learned how to relate to God's creation and to all God's creatures, how to treat everyone as a royal soul and see heaven in the ordinary chores of life; she learned the prayer of the heart and the ascetic practices of those who lived close to God, nature and the people. She learned a Christianity that enabled a person to live a fully human life.

Where was this site by the River Wear? Dr Victor Watts, a placename authority for that region, suggested two possibilities—first, a site that later became Monkwearmouth, and second, the village of Westoe, about a mile south of today's South Shields. Dr Watts suggested that the name Westoe is a compound of *stow*, meaning 'a place of assembly, a holy place' and *wifa*, the Old English genitive plural of 'woman'.[23] This name would preserve the memory of St Hilda's nuns. Westoe, however, is nearer the Tyne than the Wear, so I favour Monkwearmouth.

Bede was not interested in women. He tells us nothing about the characters and deeds of Hilda's community, apart from a few royals. Archaeology, however, does tell us something about what monastic women elsewhere in that period made, spun, and grew in their gardens. In my historical novel about Aidan[24] I let my imagination loose on that first little group of Hilda's women. I imagine them visiting local homes, bathing babies and teaching skills to the mothers, growing herbs and treating diseases, erecting guest huts and teaching people to cook, spin, write, pray, learn and tell Gospel stories, and make prayer mats. My imagination may not have been far out, for Hilda and her first group of women quickly outgrew that place, which suggests that they had great drawing power.

In 649, Heiu, the founder of the Hart's Pool monastery, withdrew to live as a solitary. The village of Healaugh, three miles from Tadcaster, is thought to be the site of her hermitage: the name was perhaps originally Heiulseg, 'Heiu's territory'. Hilda was asked to take charge of the monastery at Hart's Pool, which was already a monastery for both women and men. Built in the early Saxon style, it was probably a walled enclosure of simple wooden huts surrounding a church. A village was founded around the monastery in the seventh century, marking the earliest beginnings of the modern town of Hartlepool.[25] No trace remains of the original foundation, but its monastic cemetery has been found near the present St Hilda's Church, on Hartlepool headland.

There Hilda established a Rule of life that embodied what she had learned from Aidan and (through visits to Frankia, perhaps) other wise teachers from Ireland, such as Columbanus. Getting the Rule right was clearly fundamental, and she would have taken great pains over it. Bede stresses that establishing a Rule of life was Hilda's priority at Hartlepool: she 'began immediately to order it in all things under a rule of life, according as she had been instructed by learned men; because of her innate wisdom and love of the service of God'.

What exactly was the Rule? In one sense, the foundress was the Rule: she gave guidelines, made clear the frequency and format of daily common prayer, and set out priorities and values in her homilies. Rules at that period were generally an amalgam. Hilda's may have been influenced by her own common sense and shrewd insight, by Aidan and the Iona tradition, Columbanus and the Frankish tradition and perhaps by Gregory. It is possible that, after Hilda left Hartlepool, Roman influences were integrated: the Benedictine Rule was becoming known.

Who were the 'learned men' who frequently visited Hilda? By that time, the Lindisfarne school and scriptorium had become a major Anglo-Saxon centre of learning. The visitors were probably senior brothers who had done well in their studies at Lindisfarne, and perhaps one or two Irish brothers who had come with Aidan from Iona. They may have included one or more of the four famous brothers Cedd, Cynebil, Caelin and Chad, who became wandering scholars. If so, Cedd was the most likely to have

visited, being the eldest. Bede stresses several times that Cedd
and his brother Chad absorbed Aidan's example and traditions.

As part of her initial training, in lieu of a novitiate, Hilda may
well have visited various monasteries. Melrose, where Cuthbert
later trained and served, had a reputation for good scholarship,
which made it an ideal candidate for such a visit.

Yet Hilda, even at that stage, had to learn to work with people from
widely differing traditions. She and King Oswy's wife Enfleda most
probably spent time together, and Enfleda, reared in the Roman
tradition, desired to promote the religious life in Northumbria.
About the time that Hilda began at Hartlepool, Enfleda welcomed
to the royal headquarters at Bamburgh an outstanding 14-year-old
named Wilfrid, who was unhappy at home because of his step-
mother's unkindness. The queen sponsored a disabled nobleman
to study at Lindisfarne, and Wilfrid to be his attendant. However,
Wilfrid looked down upon the provincialism there, and soon left
for Canterbury and Rome. His influence probably took away something of the simplicity and equality that had hitherto characterised
Lindisfarne. Both Aidan and Hilda handled such difficult situations
with commendable discretion. Enfleda and Wilfrid would continue
to be woven into Hilda's life, and, although Enfleda promoted the
Roman ways, she must have been grateful to Aidan for his devoted
service as her bishop.

Double monasteries were monasteries where both women and
men lived under the rule of an abbess. It is possible that, in some
cases, they were primarily for women, the men being merely the
clerics who were needed to officiate at the services, but there is
no doubt that in the double monasteries with which Hilda was
associated, men and women played an equal part in the learning,
life and prayer of the monastery, although they had separate sleeping quarters. Bede, who knew people who had known Hilda,
refers to a monastery that had 600 'fratres': it seems that these
were tenants who lived a semi-monastic life. The Lindisfarne

monk who wrote a *Life of St Cuthbert* refers to 'a lot of servants of God who are labourers'.

During Hilda's time as abbess at Hartlepool, Bernicia become unsettled once again. For reasons unknown, the Mercian warlord Penda made two raids upon its capital, Bamburgh. Bede documents these raids in some detail, in part because, on one occasion, Aidan was on retreat on the Inner Farne Isle when Penda's warriors surrounded the royal garrison and set fire to the dwellings there. With an authority in prayer that calls to mind Christ's command to the winds and waves (Mark 4:39), Aidan raised his arm and said, 'See, Lord.' The wind changed direction, the smoke made horses or men choke, and the invaders fled. Enfleda and Oswy lived to see another day.

It is ironic that during this period, while Hilda was in Oswy's Bernicia, Aidan spent increased time in Hilda's Deira with the winsome and Christ-like King Oswin, who gave unstinting support to Aidan's mission. There was great promise in the region, in terms of spreading the faith, planting new churches and creating well-being in Hilda's homeland. The second great tragedy in Aidan's life among the English, therefore, second only to the slaughter of Oswald, was the assassination of Oswin. When it was reported that the killing had happened on the orders of Oswy, so that he could occupy Deira, the shock was so great that Aidan died within eleven days of hearing the news.

We sympathise with Aidan's final heartbreak, but what about Hilda? Her bishop and sponsor, for whom she had changed her life plan, had suffered an untimely death, and the king who had sponsored the monasteries—the husband of her relative and friend—was revealed as a power-hungry traitor. With what temptations was she assailed? The apostle Paul wrote that to those who love God, all things work together for good (Romans 8:28). So it would be for Hilda.

Reflection

To love another person is to see the face of God.
Victor Hugo, *Les Miserables*

Christianity began among a persecuted minority and spread among slaves. Its central emblem is a man dying on a cross. It places pride at the top of its list of deadly sins—and yet, the deadly sins quietly reassert themselves. Success brings power, and power corrupts. The Pharisee tendency lives on in the church and becomes endemic. Once Christianity becomes the main religion of the Roman Empire (in 380), 'empire' enters the church's soul, and Rome is its head. Magnificent buildings, glorious liturgies, hierarchies of clergy, monochrome organisation, pervasive regulations—all good or neutral in themselves—become the weapons of empire driven by the lust for power. The founder, the one who was the Son of Humanity and had nowhere to lay his head, becomes a mere image. Not only the essence of his divinity—the humility in the heart of God—is lost, but also the essence of his humanity, the warmth of a person who is true to their nature as a child of God.

Hilda and Oswald came from different parts of a network of royal Saxon families who acquired enormous wealth through violent seizures of land previously owned by Celtic Britons, as well as through trade such as the sale of wool and cloth from their landholdings. Yet they were shaped by Aidan, who renounced wealth and knew that, in order to be fully human, we have to be strict with the renegade inside ourselves.

Oswald faced a terrible situation. 'Things fall apart, the centre cannot hold' wrote the Irish poet W.B. Yeats ('The Second Coming', 1919). The world of Northumbria had fallen apart, yet that young man and his staunch band knew, having stormed the royal centre, that military might alone could not create a cohesive and contented people. They worked to repair the trust, order and prosperity that had been destroyed, by capturing the people with a vision of a better way than the old gods of power and prestige. Oswald's beautiful partnership with Aidan was an expression of the Christian faith that, unlike the mass conversions of the short-lived Roman mission, came alive in ordinary people's hearts, was lived out in common life and did not shut the God of creation in a churchy box. It also brought Hilda in from the cold.

Some marks of Aidan's (and Hilda's) mission were:

- A simple and ascetic lifestyle
- Roots in prayer and scripture
- People-friendly mission
- Churches that were villages of prayer, learning and hospitality
- An awareness of God's presence in creation and of heaven in ordinary life
- Soul friendship—the nurturing of people through gentle relationship, not insistent pressure.

What changes do we need to put in place for these to become the marks of our work and of our church today?

God of Aidan of the warming heart,
Give us the gift of generosity.
God of Aidan of simple dress,
Give us the gift of simplicity.
God of Aidan of the gentle touch,
Give us the gift of gentleness.
God of Aidan of the ceaseless prayer,
Give us the gift of prayer.
God of Aidan of the friendly greeting,
Give us the gift of meeting.

In the light of Hilda's response to Aidan, consider how you may respond to a call that God is putting upon your heart.

Wholeness:
spiritual formation
at Whitby

Hilda's great life work was accomplished at Whitby. She did not choose to go there—she was appointed—but she bloomed where she was planted. Here, a new generation of male and female Christian leaders was spiritually formed. The spirituality in which they were steeped was, in a word, wholeness.

Wholeness is the realisation of our humanity. The disparate elements within us have to be integrated around our God-given core; work, study, spiritual life, family, relationship with the earth, recreation and use of time, money and energy all have to be integrated with God in the wider world. Often, however, even if we recognise that we are part of something greater, we are unable to make the connections. Hilda made the connections.

We cannot begin the journey away from fragmentation towards wholeness until we accept our own and the world's woundedness. Hilda's move to Whitby was born of a wound. After Aidan's death, Penda attacked Oswy again, and this time the entire land was at risk. Archaeological excavations of the royal headquarters at Yeavering reveal a devastation by fire of Oswald's reconstructed quarters. The *Life of Cuthbert* by the anonymous Lindisfarne monk tells of the young Cuthbert 'dwelling in the camp of the warriors in the face of the foe'. The ninth-century historian Nennius suggests that Oswy was forced to flee to his northern border and offer Penda vast assets, including the city of Sterling, plus his son by his first Irish wife as a ransom. This availed him nothing, so Oswy had to confront an army 30 times the size of his own at a battlefield near the River Winwaed (probably Whinmoor, near Leeds). Enfleda begged him to offer to God, for use as new monasteries, the estates that he had offered to Penda as a bribe—if God would give him victory. Against all the odds, Oswy won the battle, which proved a historic turning point. Not only did it secure Northumbria as the ruling kingdom in Northern England, but it marked the defeat of the last credible pagan force in Anglo-Saxon England and enabled the conversion of Mercia to Christianity. It also sowed the seeds that would lead to the Anglo-Saxons' acceptance of Roman instead of Celtic forms of church.[26]

Oswy, who had offered his son as a ransom to Penda, now offered his one-year-old daughter Elfleda to Hilda, so Hilda became her spiritual foster mother for the rest of her life. He also handed over twelve estates where monks could engage in spiritual warfare against the powers of evil and pray for the peace of the nation. Six of these estates were in Bernicia and six were in Deira, each containing ten families. Treating God as someone to be bargained with was alien to Aidan's understanding of Christ, as it is alien to the Gospels. I expect that Hilda thought this, too, but she worked from the situation as it was to develop a model of Christianity that sought to do God's will whatever the earthly outcomes.

Bishop Finan, Aidan's successor, brought fresh energy and initiatives. He consecrated two missionary bishops, sending Diuma to the Mercians, with his see at Repton, and Cedd to the East Saxons. He either proposed or supported the king and queen's proposal that Hilda should become abbess at Whitby. Two years after Oswy's victory, she would be back in her beloved Deira as Whitby's abbess. She would turn it into the most significant monastery for men and women among the English.

Local tradition claims that Hilda stopped off at the coastal settlement of Marske on her sea journey from Hartlepool to her new post. Perhaps she prepared for her daunting task by praying in a cell, traces of which have been excavated at Marske. Whitby was then called Streanaeshalch, which means the Bay of the Beacon. About the year 370, the Roman general Theodosius had built a series of at least five strongly defended cliff-top signal towers along the coast of what is now Yorkshire. The late Frank Elgee of the Doorman Museum, Middlesbrough, thought it likely that Whitby had been the chief Roman settlement on the coast between the Tees and Flamborough Head. This cannot be proved or disproved, since several acres that could otherwise have been excavated have been lost to the sea since Roman times.

There was now a chain of monasteries established near river mouths: Jarrow (on the Tyne), Monkwearmouth (the Wear), Hartlepool (the Tees) and Whitby (the Esk). The Count de Montalembert, in his epic account of the Monks of the West (1872), states that 'of all the sites chosen by monastic architects, after that of Monte Cassino I know none grander or more picturesque than that of Whitby. It is even, in certain aspects, still more imposing than the Benedictine capital, as being near the sea.'[27] Whitby was strategic, but strategy without wholeness comes to nothing.

Some areas designated for monasteries were bleak, wild places: among the fierce elements and the shrieks of wild creatures, far from humanising dwellings, evildoers and demons of fear gained a hold. Aidan had stressed the importance of cleansing such places by praying in them for 40 days before beginning to build. His student Cedd did this at Lastingham, and I have no doubt that Hilda, too, took prayer for the healing of Whitby most seriously.

Bede twice refers to Hilda taking possession of this site without clarifying what it was. It may have been a small, struggling or Irish-led community that Oswy or Bishop Finan wished to replace or reform; their appointment of Hilda could have been a controversial or uncharitable action, which Bede skated over.

There was clearly enough land for a major expansion to take place. Recent archaeology has found, 120 metres from the monastery church, a large cemetery of men, women and children that could pre-date Hilda, so perhaps some form of religious community was already there, which Hilda put in order and extended to fill the whole headland.

In Hilda's model of church, as in personal life, the whole was greater than the parts. If Hilda began from scratch, she probably brought twelve brothers and twelve sisters or novice recruits with her. She discharged her new task with great industry and established the same Rule as at Hartlepool. Justice, devotion, purity and, above all, peace and love were the goals she put before her brothers and sisters and lay members who worked the land. Despite the fact that the community included royalty, no one was rich and no one was in need, for, suggested Bede, they followed the example of the early church in Jerusalem (Acts 4:32). They had all things in common and none held on to private property. Scripture and justice, a word of life and a way of life—these were the non-negotiable basics to which everyone who trained at Whitby committed themselves. Hilda poured spiritual care and intellectual energy into her students. She 'obliged those who were under her direction to give so much time to reading of the Holy Scriptures, and to exercise themselves so much in works of justice, that many might readily be found there fit for the priesthood and the service of the altar' (Bede, Penguin, p. 211).

From the cemetery finds, from what is known of other double Anglo-Saxon monasteries founded in the seventh century, such as Hartlepool, Ely and Barking, and from later chronicles that describe Whitby as having 40 or 50 stone cells, we can build a picture of this monastic village. The monastery was half-timbered, with stone foundations, and was divided into living and working areas. The women's cells were separate from the men's but there was a shared chapel, in which they would have met for common prayer at least five times a day, using psalms, scripture readings, litanies and silence for reflection. There was also a school where tutors taught students the Bible and theology, and a scriptorium where copies of the Gospels and other books were made.

In the scriptorium, scholars learned to write on wax tablets, which allowed the words to be erased over and again. Stylus pens for this purpose have been found. It is possible that beginners were taught using wet sand. Vellum for new copies of Gospels and psalm books was prepared in the monastery from calf skin, and parchment from sheep skin. More than 100 animals were needed to produce one Psalter. A Northumbrian Bible, now in Florence, contains over 2000 pages of vellum and weighs about 80 pounds. Thus the library became an important feature of the monastic life.

A common refectory provided meals and warmth. A great fire would be lit in the centre, with only a smoke hole in the roof, so it was necessary to light the fire many hours before it was needed (or keep it alight permanently) to allow the smoke to clear. The fire was probably always kept alight.

Beyond the monks' living quarters were fields and accommodation for those who worked the land—small rectangular huts of wood and thatch. Daily tasks would be catching fish, rearing cattle and fowl, growing cereals, gathering fruits, spinning, and making books and items for worship and the kitchens. For woodwork there were a variety of tools in use. Axes, adzes, saws and even a lathe are mentioned by Bede, and soon there must have been finer tools developed for woodcarving. In addition to the extensive workshops that surrounded the monastery, there was a separate house for the novices and a guest house.

The staple foods were meat, fish and bread. Wheat was widely grown, and its production was one of the reasons the Romans had come to Britain. Barley and oats also grew well. There was not enough grain to feed all the cattle, however. At the end of autumn many were slaughtered, and their meat was salted or smoked. Wild boar, hares and rabbits could all be caught. Cabbage was grown, and in summer there were plenty of root crops, peas and beans, while, in spring, nettles, bistort leaves and wild garlic were gathered. Even seaweed was probably soaked and made into laver-bread. Basketwork beehives were everywhere, for honey was the only form of sweetening. In summer there were also berries, apples and plums. Goats and cows provided milk and cheese. Imported spices were precious but they were necessary to disguise the taste of meat that was far from fresh. Several wells provided water and, for special occasions, they had mead, brewed from honey and barley. There was also a type of beer and wine for Holy Communion, which had to be imported. Glass vessels and fragments of windows, bangles for children and stones for sharpening knives have been found during excavations.

These excavations confirm that the monastery soon became a thriving village. In the 1920s, Sir Charles Peers discovered the foundations of several rectangular stone buildings in the area immediately north of the present abbey church. In the 1990s, English Heritage, who manage the present abbey site, carried out excavations on parts of the headland next to it. Near the cliff edge were traces of substantial timber buildings, parts of which had already fallen into the sea. On the westward slopes, overlooking the harbour, there was evidence of terracing, with numerous timber houses and enclosures. Rainwater was collected in stone-lined cisterns. Also discovered were loom weights of baked clay, which were tied to the bottom of vertical strands hung from a loom to hold them steady while the weaver threaded the weft between them. These are now displayed in Whitby Museum. A fragment of cloth and a jet spindle whorl for twisting the thread that the sisters spun are preserved in the British Museum. In 2009–2010, the laying of a pipeline in the field west of the abbey unearthed pottery and a copper alloy dress-pin from the medieval period.

Before long, abbesses or their communities had their own ships. It is not impossible that Hilda had a monastery ship anchored in Whitby harbour. Pottery evidence suggests that this important harbour had international trading links. Kings and nobles came to pray and seek advice, and the monastery, or minster (the term the English came to use), became the chief burial place for Northumbria's royalty. According to English Heritage, there would have been an enclosure around the monastic area, although no evidence of one has been found. Is it possible that Hilda insisted that the community be open, like many Irish monastic communities, which had nothing but a ditch surrounding them?

Monastic villages such as Whitby became religious, cultural and commercial centres, some even minting their own coinage. There were no towns as we know them: the monasteries *were* the towns—centres for consumption, production, exchange, and prayer.

Reflection

Community reminds us we are to love; if based on self-interest it cannot survive.

PARKER J. PALMER, *A PLACE CALLED COMMUNITY*

There would not be a body if each member was independent.

1 CORINTHIANS 12:19 (WEYMOUTH NEW TESTAMENT)

Hilda's Whitby offers us a model of true community. Today's capitalist economy has turned us into a collection of consumers—a collision of egos rather than a community. Few today are able to live together in one close-knit place, such as a monastic village, but the essential, biblical values of community may be expressed in diverse ways—for example, letting the church be a home for everyone in the area; sharing meals, produce or a listening ear; praying and caring for sick neighbours or their children.

The balance between theological study and practical service in the training of Hilda's students was holistic learning at its best, and it brought forth a fine crop of students fit to be ordained priests. We may picture them at their books in the morning and going out among the poor, illiterate villagers in the afternoons. Tall wooden crosses, forerunners of the carved stone ones which can still be seen, were beginning to be erected in the countryside, set up by mission students and sympathetic landowners to mark a convenient place for their workers to gather for prayer and instruction. The remains of a stone cross can still be seen in one of the villages near Whitby. The students must have displayed energy, creativity, discipline and love, and many others joined them. They learned to depend upon God and to get on with people while 'on the job'.

Something was lost, as well as gained, when universities were removed from the monasteries. The 'paralysis of analysis' and contempt for the non-intellectual have no place in true learning, which combines head, heart and hands, each contributing as they can.

The Community of Aidan and Hilda describe their courses as 'head through the heart learning': they are based on love of God, people and learning, not love of letters. The foundation course on its way of life, 'Igniting the flame', encourages students to learn by reflecting on scripture, creation, inspired people and experience, by using all five senses and by obedience to God.

Day by day, dear Lord:
Teach me from your Word and your world
Lead me on my pilgrimage of life
Free me to live in your rhythms
Spur me to overcoming prayer
Strip from me all that clutters
Cherish through me your creation
Heal through me what is broken
Blow me to places on the edge
Inspire me to foster unity
Reach out through me with your justice, truth and love.

FROM THE COMMUNITY OF AIDAN AND HILDA

Hilda's greatness as a scholar and mentor emerges in the life of her disciples. Bede focuses on priests, but there were others. A series of paintings on the wall of the Hilda room at Sneaton Castle Centre, Whitby, depicts scenes from the life of Hilda. In the second of these, she is surrounded by three generations of her protégés—infants, such as her relative, the baby Princess Elfleda; young students in vows; and senior citizens who sought her advice. The next picture depicts her with the illiterate cowherd Caedmon, whose songwriting she encouraged. Thus we see three generations of apprentices from all kinds of background.

From what we are told of her apprentices after they left Whitby, they would typically look for a poor or needy person in a village and help them in practical ways, pray for them, perhaps offer them training, and seek their healing and wholeness. Wholeness might mean standing up for people who were mistreated by their powerful bosses, just as Aidan and Hilda did.

No fewer than five of Hilda's students went on to become bishops, each of whom had outstanding merit and sanctity. Their names were Aetla, Bosa, John, Oftfor and Wilfrid the Younger (to distinguish him from the troublesome prelate). Then there was Tatfrid, who was appointed to be bishop of the Hwiccas (probably at Worcester) but died before the consecration could take place. We have tantalisingly little information about these godly and fruitful apprentices, but a characteristic of the two we know most about is that they gathered young people into community and became their life coaches—with wonderful results.

We know more about John, who became Bishop of Hexham in 687, than any other of Hilda's apprentices. His deacon, Berthun, personally told Bede of John's good works. Every Lent, and at other times, John would take a few companions to some secluded cells next to a burial ground in a wood opposite the River Tyne and spend time in prayer there. He asked his companions to seek out someone in one of the local villages who had a special need and invite that person to share their life together during their retreat. The 'need' might consist of acute poverty, trauma or physical or emotional illness. That was John's custom: that was Hilda's way of doing things.

On one occasion, John's companions brought a youth who was mute and had so much scurvy that no hair would grow on the top of his head. He was already known to John because he had gone to Hexham to receive alms. The bishop provided him with a cell and a daily allowance of necessities. On the second Sunday of Lent, he invited the youth to come to him and asked him to put his tongue out. He took hold of the lad's chin and made the sign of the cross on his tongue. He told him to draw the tongue back into his mouth and say something. 'Just say "Yes",' he said. The lad said, 'Yes'. The bishop started working through the alphabet: 'Say "A".' He said, 'A', and then 'B' and so on. Then the bishop asked him to repeat a word with two syllables. The lad managed this, and then he spoke a complete sentence. All that day, half the night, and through the next day, the lad not only repeated sentences but shared his inmost thoughts, which had long been trapped inside him. John asked their physician to give the lad treatment for his scurvy. A good hair of head grew and the boy grew to be handsome. The bishop invited him to join his community at Hexham, which, tellingly, Bede describes as his family—although the young man chose to go home.

In 707, Wilfrid, who had long had designs on the See of Hexham, returned from abroad and replaced John as bishop, but John never allowed enmity to develop between himself and Wilfrid. When Hilda's student Bosa died at York, John was appointed bishop in his place. He took Berthun with him to York, who founded a monastery in a forest, which is now Beverley. There John exercised an outstanding healing ministry, and is known to us as John of Beverley.

On a previous occasion, in 686, John visited a women's

monastery at a place called Wetadun (Watton-with-Beswick, in the Yorkshire Ridings). One wonders if Hilda had anything to do with that foundation, but all we know is that Hereberga was abbess. Bede describes, on the authority of an eyewitness, a wonderful cure effected on one of the nuns through John's blessing. Coenberg, the daughter of the abbess, who was a widow and was expected to succeed her mother as abbess, was crippled with bleeding and swelling and seemed likely to die. John thought she was beyond cure but, under pressure from Hereberga, agreed to pray over her. Shortly after he left, he and his party were called back and were met by a cheerful Coenberg, who looked in perfect health. She told them, 'As soon as the bishop prayed I began to mend; although my strength has not yet fully returned, the pain has left me as if the bishop carried it away with him.' Nothing further has been recorded of this convent, and it is probable that it shared in the destruction that overtook Beverley Minster and many other religious houses in Yorkshire when the Danes ravaged the north in 866.

Berthun told of a similar healing in the country house of an earl named Puch, whose wife had suffered from a condition for 40 years and had been bedbound for three weeks. The bishop had consecrated a church in the earl's grounds, and the earl asked him to eat at his house. John, who was fasting, excused himself but sent a brother to visit the earl's wife and wash the spot where the pain was greatest, with water that he had blessed for the consecration of the church. However, they wanted John in person, and eventually he agreed to go. Echoing Jesus' healing of the mother of Simon Peter's wife (Mark 1:31), when they arrived the wife was up, handed Bishop John the cup that had contained the water, and served them throughout the dinner.

On yet another occasion, after John had consecrated a church built by another earl, named Addi, the earl pleaded with him to visit his servant, who had lost the use of his limbs and was at death's door. Although the coffin was already beside the bed,

Addi told with tears how much his servant meant to him and how he truly believed that the bishop's prayer would bring a healing. As they left the room, the bishop said customary words, 'May you soon recover', and they began their meal. Soon after, the servant sent a message: 'Could I have a cup of wine?' John blessed the wine; the servant drank it, got dressed, greeted the guests and said, 'Can I enjoy the rest of the celebration with you?' Bede says that he 'drank merrily' and lived a long life.

One of John's red-blooded young clergy, named Herebald, joined in some horse-racing at a mad gallop. When the horse leapt into a large hollow, Herebald cracked his skull and broke his thumb on a rock, and lay like one dead. He could not be moved so they stretched a canopy over him and left him there from early morning until dark. They then carried him home and he lay speechless through the night. Bishop John loved him dearly, and he left the other brothers and spent the night alone in prayer for Herebald's recovery. Early in the morning, John prayed over him and asked Herebald if he knew who he was. He did. 'Can you live?' he asked. 'God willing, with your prayers,' Herebald replied. John laid hands on the broken skull. When he returned, Herebald was sitting up and able to talk. Then the bishop asked an unexpected question that is informative for us: 'Were you really baptised?' He drew out from Herebald that the priest who had baptised him had not understood the implications that this had for a transformed way of life, whereupon John took it upon himself to catechise Herebald. He had sensed that the lack of mindfulness that had led to the accident was because Herebald had not been given the whole spiritual formation that should accompany the profession of faith.

John retired for the last four years of his life to the monastery he had founded, where, Bede says, he engaged in 'holy conversation'. When he was very old, he consecrated his own apprentice, Wilfrid the Younger, as Bishop of York in his place. The year was 718. This Wilfrid is described as a very holy man who was interested in education. He embellished York Minster during his time, having silver vessels made for use at the altar and embossing the altar and the crosses with gold and silver leaf.

The younger Wilfrid is considered a saint, his feast day being 29 April, but there are only occasional mentions of him in martyrologies (lists of saints and their feast days).

Bosa was a man of sanctity and humility. When the older prelate Wilfrid was banished from the Bishopric of York in 678, Bosa was given his diocese, although it was reduced to the area of Deira. His episcopate lasted nine years. With Wilfrid back in favour, Bosa was removed in 687, only to be returned once more in 691. He had learned well the art of discipling others, taking into his household a boy named Acca, whom he mentored from an early age. He taught him (and no doubt others) to be learned in scripture, pure in his faith and observant in his devotional practices to his last days. Acca was an outstanding singer and, after leaving Bosa and joining Wilfrid, he developed new worship songs at Hexham. Bosa died on 9 March 705. He appears as a saint in an eighth-century liturgical calendar from York.

Oftfor applied himself to the study of scriptures in two of Hilda's monasteries, furthered his education with Archbishop Theodore in Canterbury and Rome, and then came back to Britain to evangelise among one of the ethnic minority people, the Hwicci. These people lived in the area now covered by Worcestershire, Gloucestershire and the western half of Warwickshire. Bede says that he not only preached but also modelled the Christian way of life. Bosel, the bishop of that province, became too ill to carry out his duties, and Oftfor was, by universal consent, chosen as bishop in his place. A little while before Bosel had been made bishop, Tatfrid, a man of great industry and learning and of excellent ability, had been chosen as bishop but had been snatched away by an untimely death before he could be consecrated. Bede states that yet another of Hilda's apprentices, Aetla, was made Bishop of Dorchester.[28] No doubt Bede could, if he had wished, have reported a glory trail of fruits in the lives of other apprentices of

Hilda who, though less suited to be bishops, were just as Christ-like.

All Hilda's students had to live under the regular common discipline of justice, devotion and purity, as well as sharing of money and possessions. This was significant because members of the royal family and the nobility were part of the monastery. They had no special favours; there were no royal perks. Three women of Hilda's extended blood family, two of them resident at Whitby, were informal 'apprentices' who came to be recognised as saints.

Some time after Aidan's death in 651, Oswy's sister Ebbe became a widow and was given the disused Roman fort on the river Derwent (about twelve miles to the south-west of Newcastle) to establish a monastery. Tradition says that, during a disruption, she was captured but escaped on a boat down the River Humber and out to sea, and established her monastery at the place now known as St Abbe's Head in Berwickshire. According to the 1510 *Breviary of Aberdeen*, she took the veil from Bishop Finan of Lindisfarne. It would be most likely that she sailed down to Whitby before she took full vows, to spend time with Hilda.

When King Oswy and Queen Enfleda dedicated their first daughter to be a bride of Christ at the age of one, as a thank-offering for victory in a battle that otherwise would have ended their lives and their kingdom, they asked Hilda to be her spiritual foster mother. Hilda began this foster care at her monastery at Hartlepool and continued it at Whitby. Hilda probably sent her to spend periods with the brothers at Lindisfarne, to learn from apprentices who had imbibed so much from the humble, listening spirit of their founder, Aidan. We can glean that Elfleda, like Hilda, was shaped by the brothers at Lindisfarne, for the anonymous Lindisfarne monk who wrote a *Life of Cuthbert* obtained first-hand information from her. So, too, did Herefrith, an abbot of Lindisfarne, who provided Bede with material for his revised *Life of Cuthbert*. Hilda mentored Elfleda until she herself became a teacher of the monastic life. Elfleda was highly esteemed by Archbishop Theodore of Canterbury, and by Saint Cuthbert, who paid her frequent visits. Theodore described her as 'the wisest lady'. Eddius, in his *Life of Wilfrid*, says, 'By her wise counsels, Elfleda was ever the best adviser and comforter of the whole province; and she did much service during the minority of Osred, her nephew, by her exertions for the promotion of peace.'

It seems that Elfleda imbibed from Hilda the Irish tradition of homely hospitality, as she used to entertain her visitors at her own table. Under her care, many missionaries and scholars were sent out. Authorities other than Bede inform us that she often made visits abroad and mingled with her own relatives. Her brothers welcomed her visits and sought her counsel. King Alfred, the youngest of these princes, was watched over by her on his deathbed. She attempted to reconcile Bishop Wilfrid and the party that was opposed to him.

The 51st Letter in the *Collection of St Boniface* is addressed to an abbess abroad, named Adolana, from 'Elfled, handmaiden of the ecclesiastical household', who commends to Adolana's care another abbess, her own pupil, who from infancy had wished to visit Rome, and asks her to give any useful information respecting the journey there. The letter had apparently been consigned to the care of Boniface on one of his journeys to the imperial city.

Once, when deprived by illness of the use of her limbs, Elfleda was cured by the girdle of St Cuthbert of Lindisfarne, which he sent to her. This girdle also cured one of the nuns of an intolerable pain in the head. Elfleda worked a winding-sheet for Cuthbert in return and sent it to him.

Elfleda outlived both Wilfrid and Cuthbert, who died in 687. She was present at Cuthbert's 'translation' into a fine shrine at Lindisfarne in 698 and wrapped him in a linen cloth. She herself died at Whitby on 8 February 714, aged 40, and was interred at Whitby alongside her parents. Hilda's tutelage had borne rich fruit.[29]

Enfleda, Elfleda's mother, would not, of course, have thought of herself as an apprentice of Hilda, for she was Hilda's senior in royal rank. She was brought up under the influence of Bishop Paulinus and, when she became Oswy's queen, she brought her own chaplain and expressed her devotion to Christ by following and promoting the liturgical practices of Paulinus and Rome. Nevertheless, she entrusted her daughter to Hilda's care and, on becoming a widow, went to live with Hilda at the Whitby monastery. Hilda must often have conversed with her about the spiritual nurture of Elfleda and consoled her after the death of Oswy. They must have conversed, too, about monastic matters and contentious issues, such as the conflicting Irish and Roman traditions and power conflicts erupting from people such as Wilfrid. Enfleda surely moved forward in her journey towards more holistic ways as a result of her partnership with Hilda.

When, in about 660, Etheldreda (the niece of Hilda's sister Hereswith) was persuaded to enter into marriage with the twelve-year-old Prince Egfrith, heir to Oswy, but nevertheless determined to keep her virginity and one day enter the religious life, she probably talked this through with Hilda, as well as her desire to establish new communities of Christians. The *Life of Saint Audrey*, a text by Marie de France, claims that Etheldreda established a church at Hexham with a group of holy servants of God. These included Owine, described as follows:

A very wise man and one with great authority… an extraordinary monk to whom God directly revealed his secrets. Saint Audrey made this man master of that church and of its religious life. Such a man was well suited to the church to teach divine worship, for he was honourable and affable and very gracious to the people… Inspired by the queen Saint Audrey, Owine had been converted, become a monk and abandoned all. He had heard many good things about Saint Chad, so he went to speak with him… and Chad received him among his friends… By direct revelation from God Owine often saw angels coming and going to Saint Chad to minister to him.[30]

Such was the spiritual atmosphere that attended those two East Anglian relatives, Etheldreda and Hilda. It was said that people honoured Etheldreda for her strict ascetic life and loved her for her grace. That surely owed something to her long conversations with her relative and sister in Christ, Hilda.

Some time after 672, Etheldreda returned to East Anglia with two nuns. After a solitary year in a cell, she founded a monastic community on the site of the present Ely Cathedral. She was known for her purity and for teaching her sisters to sew and knit as well as pray. It is said that she never wore linen but only woollen garments. She became a seer and foretold the coming of a plague, indicating how many sisters would die of it—including herself. Three days before her death in 679, a doctor made a large incision on a painful tumour under her jaw to drain away the poisonous matter, and this relieved her for a time. She nevertheless welcomed the pain, saying that as a girl she had loved to adorn herself with jewellery and necklaces, so God was allowing her, through the pain, to be released from the guilt of vanity. 'Now I wear a burning red tumour on my neck instead of gold and pearls,' she said. I wonder whether Hilda had told her the story of her own mother's vision, of a jewel in her womb. Etheldreda, like Hilda, had become a jewel of Christ.

We shall explore the story of the cowherd Caedmon in a later chapter. The Old English translation of Bede's *History of the English People* specifically notes that Caedmon's instructors themselves learned from what he spoke, and they wrote it down. This was not 'top-down' learning; it was two-way learning—the learning of the shared human journey. The instructors showed humility and forward thinking.

Caedmon' s story is unique but Hilda's approach of identifying and nurturing God-given gifts in the uneducated as well as the learned was not limited to him. At Hilda's monastery, everyone had an opportunity to find and develop their vocation, although the names and number of such people we shall never know.

Apprenticeship with Hilda was about deep inner workings of character, not just quickly acquired skills. It was an apprenticeship in waiting, patience and hiddenness. There is no suggestion that there were artificial deadlines. As the prophet Elisha waited 14 years between his call and the departure of his mentor, Elijah (1 Kings 19:19; 2 Kings 2:11)—during which he was just being around, washing the hands of the prophet, listening and watching—so, perhaps, did some of Hilda's sisters. Simply sharing the life of Hilda's community was an apprenticeship in prayer and hospitality, learning and outreach, all grounded in a Rule of Life. This produced people of such strong, faithful lifestyle that they in turn attracted others. Bede put it like this:

Thus this handmaid of Christ, the Abbess Hilda, whom all that knew her called Mother, for her singular piety and grace, was not only an example of good life, to those that lived in her monastery, but afforded occasion of amendment and salvation to many who lived at a distance, to whom the blessed fame was brought of her industry and virtue. For it was meet that the dream of her mother, Bregusuid, during her infancy, should be fulfilled... This dream was doubtless fulfilled in her daughter that we speak of, whose life was an example of the works of light, not only blessed to herself, but to many who desired to live aright.

Sadly, all records of life in the monastery after Elfleda's death have perished: for a century and a half, there is no record of its work or progress. Yet we can draw assurance from the few facts we have, that a period of creative labours followed. The fact that Bishop Trumwine and his attendants joined the monastery under its last abbess, Elfleda, held promise that, over ensuing generations, able students continued to come, even though abbesses were replaced by abbots.

Reflection

The generative forces of the world are wholesome and there is no destructive poison in them.
WISDOM 1:14

In Hilda we see an approach to making the world whole. In later centuries, rationalism disconnected the mind from the heart, industrialism disconnected people from nature, the schisms between the Roman and Reformed churches disconnected Christians from their common roots, work was separated from prayer, and education was separated from spirituality. Patriarchy distorted people's understanding of God and demeaned women. So, despite huge improvements in living conditions, public services and democratic process, something is missing—or rotten—at the heart of our society. The Community of Aidan and Hilda invites everyone to reconnect with God in the seasons and the soil, the saints and streets, the scriptures and the Spirit, the soul friends and the silence, and to embark on a journey away from fragmentation towards wholeness.

The Apprentice is one of the most gripping British TV series, although the contestants' apprenticeship is limited to a narrow business segment. Hilda apprenticed people for a whole life. In modern societies, the different facets of holistic apprenticeship cannot all be provided from within one local faith community. Schools, travel and the internet mean that we are shaped by disparate influences. We can, however, adopt a Rule (or Way) of Life and the habit of daily reflection, be transparent with a mentor, and journey through today's kaleidoscopic society in the spirit of Hilda's apprentices, touching base at a mother house in a place such as Whitby.

- Hilda bloomed where she was planted. Jesus said, 'I am the vine... Those who abide in me and I in them bear much fruit' (John 15:5). What might it mean for us to bloom where we are planted?
- The playwright George Bernard Shaw thought that people only work for something. In Hilda's spirituality, work has its own value, which frees the worker to be present to the moment. Reflect on work in your milieu: what may you learn from Hilda's approach?
- What do you learn from the lives of Hilda's apprentices?
- Imagine one of the aged John of Beverley's 'holy conversations' with a brother, a visitor or God, and write it down.

Source of our being and goal of our longing,
give us wisdom to harvest our life
and find the wholeness of memory.
We bring to you disjointed areas of our lives—
visit them and join them up.
Let evangelism and social care,
teaching and healing,
work and prayer—
flowing from you, their common source—
become a seamless garment of praise in all our ways.

5

Unity in diversity:
the same jewel under Irish and Roman frameworks

In 664, Whitby became the setting for one of the defining episodes in the establishment of the English church—the Synod of Whitby. King Oswy called the synod to decide whether Northumbria should follow the practices of Rome instead of Iona, in particular the date on which Easter should be celebrated. In order to consolidate his pre-eminent role among English rulers, he needed the support of other kingdoms (such as Kent, who took their instructions in church matters from Rome) and the influence that came from greater contact with the continent. That had doubtless been a factor in Oswy's choice of a queen (Enfleda) from Kent. She observed the Roman calendar with vigour, and one result was that, in some years, her Lenten fast would clash with the King's Easter banquet. Oswy therefore called a synod where a delegation from each tradition could argue their case, after which he would decide which tradition all of Northumbria should henceforth observe.

Many scholars suspect that his mind was set before the synod began, perhaps influenced by his power-hungry son Alchfrith, but it was important that he was perceived to have given each side equal rights in the debate. He still needed the support of the Irish Christian kingdom of Dalriada, and his bishops were still appointed by Iona. The setting of this crucial and controversial synod was also important if he was not to lose the support of one side or the other before it began. He therefore asked Abbess Hilda to host the synod at Whitby. It is a tribute to Hilda's status as a spiritual mother to people from both traditions, and to her organisational ability, that Oswy asked her to undertake this task. He knew he could rely upon her.

The guests began to arrive. The present and the future king came to stay. Bishop Agilbert of the West Saxons, whom they had invited to stay in Northumbria, came as head of the pro-Roman delegation. His chief spokesman was Wilfrid, then abbot of Ripon, aided by another priest named Agatho. Queen Enfleda sent her chaplain Romanus, and there was another priest named James. Bishop Colman of Lindisfarne, who led the debate for the Irish side, came to stay with his own chosen delegation.

Accommodating these guests must have challenged the monastery to its limits. Not long after his appearance at Whitby, Wilfrid would refuse to be consecrated a bishop on Northumbrian soil because he thought that those in the Irish tradition were too cavalier in their observance of the minutiae of canon law. Instead, he would be consecrated on the continent by three bishops in full regalia, and he would instruct nine priests to carry him aloft on a throne. No doubt Wilfrid made his accommodation requirements at Whitby quite clear!

It is unlikely that Colman and his party, reared in the simple style of Aidan, complained about their food or rooms. Bede wrote of 'the great frugality and austerity practised by Colman and his predecessors... They owned no wealth apart from their livestock, since any money they received from the rich was at once given to the poor. They had no need to save money or provide accommodation in order to receive the rulers of the world... and were so free from any taint of avarice that none accepted grants of land and endowments' (OUP, p. 161). These guests may have been oblivious to niceties that meant much to others. I have no doubt that Hilda would have accorded each guest equal dignity and offered everyone a warm, prejudice-free and well-ordered welcome.

Bishop Cedd arrived as the official translator. He had trained at Lindisfarne but had worked under the Roman framework of the East Saxons, whose ruler, King Sigeberht, Hilda's royal East Anglian relatives perhaps supported. Cedd had gone to the East Saxons partly as an emissary of the Northumbrian monarchy. Sigeberht's baptism (in Northumbria, by Bishop Finan of Lindisfarne) and the re-evangelisation of his kingdom had taken place on Oswy's initiative. After making some initial conversions, Cedd reported back to Finan at Lindisfarne, who ordained him bishop to the East Saxons, calling in two other Irish bishops to assist at the rite.[31] Cedd was unafraid to confront the powerful. He excommunicated one of the king's client landowners, who was in an unlawful marriage. When Sigeberht himself continued to visit the man's home, Cedd descended on their revels to denounce the king openly, foretelling that he would die in that very house. Bede asserted that the king's subsequent murder (in 660) was his penance for defying Cedd's injunction.

The proceedings of the synod were hampered by the participants' mutual incomprehension of each other's languages, which probably included Gaelic, Old English, Frankish and Early Welsh, as well as Latin. Cedd was a conscientious interpreter for both sides. His facility with the languages, together with his status, made Bede liken his role to that of the Holy Spirit at Pentecost who enabled people of diverse languages to understand Peter's words.

King Oswy presided at the synod, and Colman, Bishop of Northumbria, was the chief spokesman for the Celtic tradition. The intended main speaker for the Roman side was to have been Agilbert, second Bishop of Dorchester (of the West Saxons), but Agilbert was a Frank (later to be Bishop of Paris) and couldn't make himself understood in English, so he asked Wilfrid to speak in his place.[32]

The clinching argument for Oswy, according to Bede, came when Wilfrid asserted the following: 'Although your Fathers were holy men, do you imagine that they, a few men in a corner of a remote island, are to be preferred before the universal Church of Christ throughout the world? When,' Wilfrid asked, 'did Jesus say to Columba, as He had said to Peter: "... I tell you, you are Peter, and on this rock I will build my church, and the gates of Hades will not prevail against it. I will give you the keys of the kingdom of heaven?"'

'Is this true?' Oswy asked Colman. 'Did Jesus never say similar words to Columba?' Colman admitted that he had not. 'Then, I tell you,' Oswy decided, 'Peter is the guardian of the gates of heaven, and I shall not contradict him. I shall obey his commands in everything to the best of my knowledge and ability; otherwise, when I come to the gates of heaven, there may be no one to open them, because he who holds the keys has turned away.'

It seems that the debate was one-sided and, in terms of eloquence and skilful presentation, the Irish were outclassed and outmanoeuvred.

Yet Bede records that Hilda and her followers were for the Irish side of the argument. Why? I doubt whether Hilda was intellectually convinced by either Colman's or Wilfrid's arguments, both of which were faulty. Neither the Irish Easter tradition (followed by the entire Western church until Rome changed it) nor the Roman tradition was followed by the first-century apostles. The Irish position was, however, held in good faith. It is more likely that Wilfrid's grandiloquent smokescreen repelled Hilda. Did she sense that he wanted the Roman Easter not because he loved truth or unity, but because he was in love with pomp and power?

The 'presenting issue' of the conflict was the dating of Easter. The problem arose from attempts to map a festival whose origins are in the Jewish lunar calendar on to the Roman solar calendar. It is possible to fix the date by astronomical observation, as is done today for the Islamic festivals of Ramadan and Eid, or it is possible to fix the date by mathematical calculations, based on tables of astronomical observations. These tables, depending on their accuracy, could throw up repeating cycles of 8, 11, 19 and 84 years. The churches at Alexandria and Antioch used different tables. It was the Antioch version that was used in the native churches in Celtic lands, brought back to Britain by bishops who had attended the Council of Arles in AD314. Britain and Ireland were content with this system of calculating Easter, even when new, more accurate tables, based on a 19-year cycle, were produced. The new system was adopted by the Roman church, and Pope Leo the Great (440–461) sent out an edict to that effect—which didn't reach Britain or Ireland because communication was slower and more difficult in those days. King Oswy, brought up in Celtic Dalriada, kept Easter according to the Celtic 84-year cycles, but his wife Enfleda, daughter of the Queen of Kent, followed the Kentish (Roman) cycle of 19 years.

In the time of the apostles, it must have seemed so simple. God had told the Jews to celebrate the Passover on the first Friday after the first full moon after the spring equinox, so the early Christians celebrated Christ's resurrection on the first Sunday after the first full moon of the Spring equinox. As time went by, Christians in the capital city of the Roman Empire disliked the fact that, occasionally, Easter Sunday came before the Jewish Passover. Anti-Semitism had begun to rear its ugly head in Rome (the Irish were not anti-Semitic: they knew no Jews). If that was an unacknowledged factor, Hilda would have wanted none of it. An acknowledged factor was that it made more administrative and symbolic sense for Easter always to come after Passover. Instead, however, of simply making that point, the proponents felt it necessary to justify it by arguing that this had the authority of the chief of the apostles. I doubt if Hilda had sympathy for such 'gerrymandering theology'. Perhaps the main reason why she supported the Irish side was that the Irish mission had introduced a spirituality of integrity—in relationship to God, people, creation and the church. She herself was committed to this. She had seen the fault-lines in the Roman approach in her childhood. She dreaded losing the Irish spirituality.

Whatever her reasons for siding with the losing Irish side, it took courage. She owed her position to the royals who wanted to go over to Rome. It was to her political advantage to abstain, at least, but she voted according to her conscience, without fear or favour. It was surely this quality that contributed to the honour in which she was held by both sides.

Much more lay behind the synod than the date of Easter, however. For example, from that time, the Northumbrian kingdom adopted the Roman tonsure for monks. The monks now had to shave off their long back hair, which had been the joy of Celtic men. There were many other new regulations, of which we have no details: Bede records that the brothers that remained at Lindisfarne complained much about them. It is clear that a whole new way of 'doing church' had been imposed

The two sides in this dispute are often stereotyped. The synod is presented as a choice between being linked with the universal catholic church or being independent, in which case the decision in favour of Rome, it is claimed, was right and inevitable. I think this is a false reading of the issue. The Irish Christians thought of themselves as catholic Christians and loyal members of the universal church, acknowledging its primacy. They believed, however (erroneously), that their practices in regard to Easter originated with the apostle John, just as the Roman party claimed (erroneously) that their practices originated with Peter. Bishop Colman stated his view that the Irish custom was 'the same which the blessed John the Evangelist, the disciple specially beloved of our Lord, with all the churches over which he presided, is recorded to have celebrated'. It is still the case that the Eastern Church dates Easter differently from the Western Church (though not using the same formula as the Celtic churches), yet that did not prevent Pope John Paul II and the Ecumenical Patriarch in

Istanbul from exploring how their two ecclesial bodies might evolve into closer communion.

I think the most crucial underlying issue was the use and abuse of power in deciding what matters should be determined by the centre and what matters were best left for local decision. The Second Vatican Council (1962–65) called for a plurality of cultures within the church and of inculturation within different countries. The gospel requires all Christians to respect and honour one another. The way in which changes are brought about is as important as the changes themselves. At the time of the Whitby Synod, the Irish felt an affinity with John and the eastern churches. They lived the gospel in a natural, intuitive way: the stiffness of the Latin church's regulations was alien to them. They saw no conflict between what was good in their culture and the way of Christ. They were also close to God in creation. To them it must have seemed nonsense to celebrate the resurrection of Christ, the light of the world, before the spring equinox, on a day when there was more darkness than light.

All of Lindisfarne's Irish monks and 30 of their English brothers were so distraught at the change that they left for Ireland via Iona. Did Hilda know they would do this before the synod concluded? Whether she did or not, she must have been devastated by their decision. Although various bishops and monastic leaders trained by Aidan remained in post after the synod, it marked the approaching end of Iona's oversight. The new oversight, however, although it adopted the Roman framework and was pressured by people such as Bishop Wilfrid, also included people like Hilda at Whitby, Chad in Mercia and Cuthbert, who was put in charge at Lindisfarne. They sustained Aidan's spirituality under the new framework with the same integrity and self-giving as before.

The decade that ensued saw conflicts in church and state. Whitby seems to have been an anchor of calm amid a sea of storms. If Hilda had been a lesser woman, she could have been sucked into partisan bickering. A generational conflict grew between the ageing Oswy and his Irish-born son Alchfrith, who possibly led a short-lived uprising in Deira. Alchfrith seems to have been the prime mover in making Wilfrid a bishop over the entire area of Northumbria. A year after the synod. Wilfrid turfed out leaders trained in the Irish mission and threw his weight around wherever he could, with enormous energy, accumulating huge areas of land but with scant regard to Christian charity or teamwork.

Oswy died in 671 and was succeeded by his Northumbrian-born son Egfrith, whose mother Enfleda retired to the monastery at Whitby. She was used to having her way. She had promoted Wilfrid and she would succeed Hilda as abbess. The monastery would be dedicated to Saint Peter: no doubt Enfleda, if not Oswy, insisted on this as a sign that it should follow in the steps of Peter's Rome rather than Columba's Iona. It can't have been easy for Hilda, and yet there is no hint of bad feeling between them.

In 668, a statesmanlike new Archbishop of Canterbury, Theodore, was appointed. He strove to unite the diverse church traditions of the English kingdoms. After Egfrith became king, Theodore, supported by Egfrith, proposed that Northumbria should have several smaller dioceses. The bishops chosen for these sees were Eata at Hexham, Eadhaed at Lindsey (which was more or less annexed to Northumbria) and Bosa at York. Eata had been trained by Aidan but Wilfrid had expelled him from Ripon, and, of course, Hilda had trained Bosa at Whitby.

Wilfrid disliked these nominees since they did not come from his foundations. He went to Rome to appeal against Theodore's and Egfrith's decisions, thus becoming the first Englishman to challenge a royal or ecclesiastical decision by petitioning the papacy. Hilda exercised her own leadership: despite the fact that she was unwell, she sent a representative to put the case for Bosa, who, she felt, was being trampled on by Wilfrid.

As Enfleda's protégé, Wilfrid gained more power, but he overreached himself. Power corrupts. He left a trail of wrecked human relationships as long as his trail of new foundations and glorious church artefacts. Rulers began to feel threatened by him. Did the two women, Enfleda and Hilda, talk through honest disagreements and wise courses of action in relation to these issues and aggrieved parties?

Pope Agatho held a synod in October 679 (mainly to deal with the Monothelete controversy, about the nature of Christ), which, although it ordered Wilfrid's restoration to the smaller diocese of York and the return of the monasteries to his control, also directed that the new dioceses should be retained. Wilfrid was, however, given the right to replace any bishop to whom he objected in the new dioceses. In 680, he returned to Northumbria and appeared before a royal council. He produced the papal decree ordering his restoration, but Egfrith tore it up and briefly imprisoned Wilfrid. Soon after his release, Wilfrid went to the South Saxons (Sussex) and energetically evangelised them.

Throughout this time, the basis of Hilda's action was common sense, informed by a concern that the church should be just in its dealings. She was not afraid to stand up for people who were being misrepresented, yet she took a stand in such a way that people on all sides acknowledged her spiritual authority. She bore no grudges and eschewed prejudices and judgmental words. She had truly become a transcultural spiritual mother— and, despite the Pope, three good men assumed leadership of their new dioceses.

Eddius Stephanus's biography of Wilfrid is an unremitting eulogy of his hero.[33] Yet, despite the fact that Hilda stood up to Wilfrid, Eddius refers to her with utmost respect as 'holy mother'. This can only be because she treated everyone with respect and love, without a trace of belittlement. People knew that when she stood up to them, it was not to get her own way or nurse a bruised ego; it was because she wanted the best for them as well as for the person they were treating badly. She wanted them to live as they were meant to, in accordance with gospel values.

Archbishop Theodore wrote to Elfleda, asking her to befriend

Wilfrid when he was recalled from exile by her brother, King Alchfrith. The king again quarrelled with Wilfrid but, on his deathbed, he sent for Elfleda and she declared afterwards at a council of prelates that her brother, in his last hours, had desired a reconciliation. Wilfrid, too, died a good death.

Reflection

'If a kingdom is divided against itself, that kingdom cannot stand.'
MARK 3:24

On his last night on earth, Jesus prayed that all believers would be one as he was one with God the Father (John 17:20–21). The apostle Paul calls us to think of the universal church as a single human body with many parts, all working together for the common good (1 Corinthians 12:12–27). He urges that we be eager to maintain the unity of the Spirit, for 'there is one body and one Spirit… one Lord, one faith, one baptism' (Ephesians 4:4–5). Acts 15 records how Christians settled their disagreements by meeting together in a council. Irenaeus, who led the Celtic congregation at Lyons in the traditions of the apostle John, affirmed both that 'where the Church is, there also is the Spirit of God' and that 'where the Spirit of God is, there is the Church and the fullness of grace'.[34] Such a voice was absent at the Whitby Synod.

In his 1995 Encyclical on Christian Unity, *Ut Unum Sint*, Pope John Paul II asked Christians of other communions to forgive him, as a representative of all popes, for some of his predecessors' terrible abuses of their calling. Unity, he reminds us, 'is the fruit of an ongoing conversion of heart and purification of memories, and we are called to re-examine together our painful past'.[35] Such a voice was also absent at the Whitby Synod.

Anglican priestly orders were declared 'null and void' by one of John Paul II's predecessors (Pope Leo XIII), even though they had been ordained by the very bishops he had recognised. No such declaration has ever been made by the bishops of all branches of the church, Eastern and Western, meeting together to discern the Holy Spirit's mind on such a matter. Is it not time to reconcile these ministries?

It seems that Hilda imbibed the spirit of unity in diversity and respected 'the dignity of difference'.[36] Mary Tanner, a member of the Anglican–Roman Catholic International Commission, has written:

If God unites, ought not the world see in us a unity which is not uniformity, but also a multiplicity which is not limitless pluralism? A diversity in which the gospel is lived in each place authentically in the bodies, skins, dances, languages and thought-forms of that place? The essence of catholicity is not the imposition of a particular limited cultural norm on everyone by some central super Church, but the ability of each local Church to recognise and delight in every other community as an authentic form of the one universal Church. And this is why our cultural and ethnic differences are gifts God gives to us and which we are called to offer one another... If we could live together in a visible unity bearing the cost of differences, never again saying to one another 'I have no need of you', we should show a model of living and loving which is grounded in that mysterious Trinitarian life at whose heart is forever a cross.[37]

Hilda is regarded by the Roman Catholic church as a saint. Eulogy wrote that the saints of east and west 'have in their lives accomplished the union of the churches. Are they not citizens of the same holy and universal church? At the level of their spiritual life they have gone beyond the walls which divide us, but which... do not reach up to heaven.'[38] In quoting Eulogy, author Donald Allchin adds, 'Not only in the lives of the great saints... but wherever the life of prayer is being truly and authentically lived, there the unity of the church is being made known, through the healing action of the Holy Spirit.' The Community of Aidan and Hilda Way of Life calls us to repent of the schisms that have occurred between the Eastern and Western churches and from the Reformation onwards, to weave together the God-given strands of Christianity that later became separated, and to look upon all fellow Christians 'not as strangers but pilgrims together'.

Reflecting on the Synod of Whitby, Wendy Ward, a New Zealand Benedictine, has written:

The image of mending comes to mind... I wonder whether the Holy Spirit is arranging a worldwide sewing bee to mend the tear in the Bride's gown! It seems that Celtic Christianity has come out of a lengthy hibernation. This could mean another Synod of Whitby situation arising with a reversal of the original decision this time. I was once happy to make the most of the Benedictine tradition which takes its identity from the Roman Church. Now I believe that each tradition has gifts to offer the other so that both may be enriched.[39]

- How may you welcome Christ in different traditions?
- How might you weave together God-given strands within Christianity that have become separated?

Divine Weaver, we rejoice in the many-coloured tapestry
which is your church.
We grieve with you at the strands that have been neglected and torn.
Weave together through us
scriptural holiness and a catholic spirit,
pentecostal callings and contemplative calm,
radical justice and sacramental grace,
that we may reflect your Body on earth as it is in heaven.

6

Awakening the song in every heart:
Caedmon

Although the Irish and the Roman missions had spread the faith widely in Northumbria, the scriptures and the monastery church services were in Latin, the language that only educated people used. Hilda, however, like Aidan, had a deep commitment that the faith should be planted in the hearts of all the people. That is why she trained her students to go out into the villages, and that is why she responded so wholeheartedly to the unusual experience of one of her cowherds, Caedmon. As a result, this uneducated farm labourer, who suffered from a low self-image, became a primary evangelist of the unlettered English through his gospel songs, and was the first Anglo-Saxon poet of stature. This is how it happened.

In Hilda's village of God they had social evenings, when people gathered in a barn around a large log fire: the church, not the pub, hosted the 'karaokes' of those days. Caedmon's name suggests that he was Celtic British, not Saxon, as were many of the less well-educated population. He would live in a house of his own making, with wattle walls, turf roof and earth floor. He would most probably tend his patch of beans and fruit trees, feed his geese, hunt otter and beaver in the river, fish for eels and check his salmon traps set in the shallow tidal waters of the River Esk. He would gather honey from his hillside beehive and brew his mead from it. As a free man, he was entitled to gather timber and hunt in the forest. With his axe and knife, he would shape the wood to his everyday needs. He had his herdsman's crook and spear, buckets and barrels for storage and carrying, spades and mattocks for his work on the land, stools, shelves and plates. From the animal skins, he would make jerkins, shoes and thongs. A tusk would provide him with a horn to drink from or to blow in the forest, to reveal his whereabouts when he was walking or hunting. Animal teeth made good beads and gaming pieces, and antlers could be whittled into ornaments, spoons and needles for stitching his homemade wool and leather garments. Further away was pastureland where he worked with the cows. It is easy to imagine animals grazing the cliff-tops up towards High Whitby. Day and night, herdsmen would stand guard against predators and thieves, sleeping in the open or in crude shelters.

So Caedmon was self-sufficient—but he was shy. That is why, one evening when he found himself in the great, warm hall and his turn approached to be handed the five-stringed harp and sing something, he slid out into the darkness and returned to the stable where he guarded the cows by night. As he slept, he dreamed that a young man greeted him and said, 'Caedmon, sing me something.' 'I cannot sing,' he answered. 'That is why I left the feast and returned here.' 'If you can't sing in front of that crowd, you must sing to me,' said the young man. 'What should I sing about?' Caedmon asked. 'Sing about the beginning of creation,' said the other. Caedmon straightaway found himself singing verses he had never heard before, in praise of the Creator, the gist of which (though their beauty and loftiness is lost in translation) was as follows:

Now we must honour the guardian of heaven,
the might of the architect, and his purpose,
the work of the father of glory,

as he, the eternal lord, established the beginning of wonders;
he, the holy creator, first made heaven as a roof for mortal people.
Then the guardian of humankind,
the eternal lord, afterwards appointed the middle earth,
the lands for humans, the Lord almighty…

Awaking from his sleep, Caedmon, to his surprise, remembered all that he had sung in his dream and added more verses that worthily expressed the praise of God. The memory remained so vivid that he told his foreman. He, a man of insight, escorted Caedmon to Mother Hilda to tell her of the gift Caedmon had received. After listening to their story, Hilda called together her teachers and advisers and encouraged Caedmon to sing his verses before them, in order that they might discern the nature and origin of this gift. They all agreed that heavenly grace had been granted to him by the Lord. They expounded to him a passage of sacred history or doctrine, enjoining upon him, if he could, to put it into verse. Having undertaken this task, he went away, and returning the next morning, gave them the passage he had been bidden to translate, rendered in excellent verse. Hilda, joyfully recognising the grace of God in him, instructed him to leave his farm work and take monastic vows, but as a lay brother who would not be weighed down with Latin and theological studies that would distract from his unique calling.

Caedmon was, however, taught the Bible and sacred history. Bede describes at length how he memorised and ruminated on the Bible stories, turning them into harmonious verse and so sweetly singing it that his teachers became his listeners. He sang about the creation of the world, the origin of human beings, the history of Genesis, the departure of the children of Israel out of Egypt, their entrance into the promised land and many other histories from Holy Scripture; the incarnation, passion and resurrection of our Lord, and his ascension into heaven, the coming of the Holy Spirit, and the teaching of the apostles. Likewise he composed many songs concerning the terror of future judgment, the horror of the pains of hell, the joys of heaven, the blessings and the judgments of God, by all of which he endeavoured to draw people away from the love of sin, and to excite in them devotion to well-doing and perseverance therein. For he was, says Bede, 'a very religious man, humbly submissive to the discipline of monastic rule, but inflamed with fervent zeal against those who chose to do otherwise'.

Hilda was an extremely busy woman; she had to combine what today we might call three jobs: principal of a theological college, chief administrator of a large estate, and consultant to all kinds of people from the wider world. Yet, to her eternal credit, she took seriously this report of Caedmon's experience. Hilda recognised that God had given him a gift; she was also wise enough to realise that to have made him a Latin-learning monk would have killed it off. His calling, she said, was not to do academic studies but to compose songs of Bible stories. Caedmon's songs travelled far into the memories of people who never read a book.

It says much for Hilda that a man like Caedmon, so different from the Latin students who became bishops, flourished within the community. He was able to relax and be his humorous self. He lived to a good age, and was unwell for only the two weeks prior to his death.

Towards the end of his life, Caedmon lived near the hospice to which those likely to die were carried. One evening, he asked his carer to take him there for a rest. The carer wondered why, since there was no sign of his approaching death. They laid him down and he happily conversed with other residents until past midnight, when he asked if they had the Eucharist there. 'Why do you need the Eucharist?' they asked. 'You are not going to die yet—you talk so merrily with us, as if you were in good health.' 'Nevertheless,' said Caedmon, 'bring me the Eucharist.' Having received it, he asked whether they were all in charity with him, and had no complaint against him, nor any quarrel or grudge. They answered that they were all in perfect charity with him, and free from all anger; and in their turn they asked him to be of the same mind towards them. He answered at once, 'I am in charity, my children, with all the servants of God. Then strengthening himself with the last Eucharist before heaven, he prepared for the entrance into another life, and asked how near the time was when the brothers should be awakened to sing the nightly praises of the Lord. They answered, 'It is not far off.' Then he said, 'It is well, let us await that hour', and, signing himself with the Holy Cross, he laid his head on the pillow, and falling into a slumber for a little while, so ended his life in silence.

Friendship, humour, sacrament, praise, silence—these qualities marked the community that Hilda inspired.

Others attempted to compose religious poems after Caedmon, but none could equal him, writes Bede, 'for he did not learn the art of poetry from men, neither was he taught by man, but by God's grace he received the free gift of song, for which reason he never could compose any trivial or vain poem, but only those which concern religion' (OUP, p. 214).

Most of Caedmon's poetry is now lost or, where it survives, has been rewritten by later poets into different dialects. The Anglo-Saxons handed down their history and traditions by word of mouth. Just as the Celtic peoples did, at gatherings of kings and nobles a bard would sing of the great deeds of past heroes, adding new songs in honour of his lord. *Beowulf*, which was perhaps composed during the following century, either in Britain or Scandinavia, came down to us in this way. In these poems important points were re-stated in different words, giving rise to a wealth of synonyms characteristic of modern English. Traditional phrases recurred like a refrain. Each line had four stressed syllables, with the most important stress coming after the halfway point.

Emily Thornbury, in her chapter on Aldhelm, Abbot of Malmesbury (d. 709)[40] observes that the Anglo-Saxon/Germanic poetic tradition 'viewed the most important component of poetry as skilful technique, rather than loftiness of theme'. The idea of divine inspiration of content was alien to this tradition. Even Christians like Aldhelm, who was a poet and scholar of Latin Anglo-Saxon literature, did not expect God to provide poets with new subject matter for their poems. Thornbury is therefore fascinated by 'a very peculiar feature of Bede's narration of the Caedmon miracle: Bede's observation that Caedmon composed "with the greatest sweetness and compunction"'. She explores the multiple meanings of the Latin word for 'compunction' and concludes that Bede thought Caedmon's poems were both inspired and inspiring: they were caused by and also generated in others inspiration from God's Holy Spirit. They brought an inner compunction, a penitence and desire to serve God in others—and all this despite the fact that Caedmon knew nothing of poetic technique before he wrote his first song.

Although only Bede's record of part of one song by Caedmon survives, we know that his songs became popular far beyond the boundaries of Northumbria. From the time of Caedmon's songs, Christianity took root and shaped the traditions and values of the peasants as well as the aristocracy. That is why Caedmon's songs, and Hilda who enabled them, have a lasting place in English history.

We often tell the story of Caedmon but it might repay us to consider how, because of Hilda's listening and enabling, it led to the conversion of English poetry and, through that, to the conversion of the English imagination and people. Bede gives us a list of Caedmon's compositions (though not including their content). They cover the whole range of biblical and doctrinal topics. Before Caedmon were what Bede dismisses as frivolous and course songs; after him grew a new tradition of faith songs.

The finest flower of what some have termed the Caedmon school of poetry, and one of the oldest works in English, is *The Dream of the Rood*. This is preserved in the tenth-century manuscript housed in the Capitulary Library, Vercelli, in northern Italy. Known as the *Vercelli Book*, it is an anthology of Old English prose and verse, containing 23 prose homilies and a prose *Life of Saint Guthlac* interspersed with six poems.

A part of *The Dream of the Rood* can also be found inscribed on the Ruthwell Cross (now in the Scottish County of Dumfries). During Hilda's time, a Christian community developed there in the far north-west of Northumbria. They erected (perhaps as early as 665, or perhaps the following century) a 5.5-metre standing cross that may have been intended as a tool for the conversion of the surrounding population. Respected scholars debate whether the author of *The Dream of the Rood* was Caedmon himself or a later poet such as Bishop Cynewulf of Lindisfarne, within the 'Caedmon school' of poetry. 'Rood' is from the Old English word *rod*, meaning 'pole' or, more specifically, 'crucifix'. This cross is pictured as a tree, since the two crossbeams could have been cut from one tree: Christ himself 'bore our sins in his body on the tree' (1 Peter 2:24, RSV).

In the poem, the narrator has a dream in which he speaks to the tree. In part two, the crucifixion story is told from the perspective of the tree. The tree learns that it is not to be the bearer of a criminal but of the Son of God. The Lord and the cross become one, and they stand together as victors, refusing to fall, taking on insurmountable pain for the sake of humankind. In a sensational and culture-changing image, Christ, the blood-drenched victim, becomes the supreme Anglo-Saxon warrior who, by choosing death, makes possible eternal life for everyone. So, in Hilda's land of blood-soaked killing fields, the tree of death becomes the tree of life.

As well as Caedmon's hymns, other compositions flourished in Whitby. During the post-Hilda period, various *Lives* were written at Whitby. These included a *Life* of Hilda, now lost, and the first ever *Life* of Rome's Bishop Gregory the Great, the promoter of Augustine's mission to the English. This was the first book to be written in English. One scholar has remarked of the author of Gregory's *Life*, 'The monk compiling this is intellectually aware and creative, fusing the learned sources with the native tradition… Even on the meagre data we have it is clear that Hilda created an atmosphere of intellectual excitement and stimulus.'[41] No doubt, many other things were written, which were destroyed by the Viking invaders. Those who wrote them could draw material from the fine library, which included works by Augustine, Gregory, Jerome and others that we cannot now identify. Aldhem's works were probably there, since Elfleda refers to them in one of her letters. Visitors from Northumbria and abroad would have donated valuable books.

Whitby became a stable centre of royal, spiritual and literary power. It was a place of learning, prayer and work, a place of connections, where *Lives* of saints were written, vocations were fostered and kings and their families were buried.

The vision of unlocking the song in a shy person's heart has not faded. The Revd Dr June Boyce-Tillman MBE, Professor of Applied Music at the University of Winchester, travels the world talking about music as well-being, including the spiritual dimension in areas such as education, liturgy and healing. She explores Hilda's story in *Celtic Twilight*, a performance based on extensive research into the life of Hilda, including the versification of Celtic texts. The piece falls into five sections, involving the audience in moving, singing and creating sounds. It starts with water that flows freely, and this is linked with Hilda's birth. This leads to sharp and piercing fire at her conversion, as adolescence approaches, reflecting her energy in founding and running three religious houses. Earth represents the descent into chaos, which, for Hilda, was at the Synod of Whitby, when she lost the battle to retain the indigenous traditions of Celtic Christianity. Roman uniformity prevailed and she had to accept it without turning her community into a group of dissenters like Bishop Colman. Her work at Whitby in nurturing and teaching is linked with the lightness of air, and her final illness leads her to the silent place of death. Thus Hilda's story is used in June Boyce-Tillman's one-woman presentation as a way of illuminating issues in the contemporary world (particularly the valuing of diversity) and exploring our own inner spirituality.

June also does workshops on 'Releasing the Musician Within' and writes inclusive hymns published by the Hildegard Press and the Association for Inclusive Language. The first and last verses of one of her Hilda-inspired hymns, to the tune 'St Columba', are:

Embrace the universe with love,
And shine with God in splendour.
Embrace the earth, embrace the sky
and find God, our defender.

So even death when joy is deep
Can be Christ's benediction.
Creator-God, we sing your praise,
Like Hilda, seek your vision.

Reflection

We are God's poem.

EPHESIANS 2:10 (PARAPHRASE)

'It's never too late to find a voice.'

FROM *IT'S NEVER TOO LATE* (DIR. MICHAEL MCCARTHY, 1956)

The Community of Aidan and Hilda uses the story of Caedmon as a parable: our calling is to release the song in every human heart. The Creator has designed us to reflect the divine creativity. At the core of our being is a creative flow, which can take as many expressions as there are people.

Think of ways in which people do or could 'unlock the song that is in every human heart'.

Caitlin Matthews suggests that the skill of the Celtic poet is to bring the soul to the point of vision, rest, and stillness. The music of this healing skill is known by three 'strains': the laugh strain, which raises the spirits; the sorrow strain, which causes the release of tears; and the sleep strain, which brings rest to troubled souls.

Rowan Williams has identified four things that poetry achieves. It takes us into the realm of myth, with stories and symbols lying so deep that they give points of reference for plotting our ways in the inner and outer world. It clothes ordinary experience with extraordinary words so that we can see the radiance in the ordinary and celebrate. Through satire, it gives us a sideways glance on familiar ways of talking, behaving or exercising power, so that we are not bewitched by what looks obvious and wants us to think it's obvious. Fourthly, through lament, it gives us ways of looking at our losses and our failures that save us from despair and apathy.[42]

Storytelling is part of our Judeo-Christian heritage. The *Haggadah*, the Hebrew service book used in Jewish households on Passover Eve at a festive meal to commemorate the exodus from slavery in Egypt, literally means 'narration'. Its purpose was to enthral the young, providing education through entertainment. The *Golden Haggadah*, an extended version made in Spain in 1320, includes poems and pictures.

Andy Freeman writes, 'The arts and creativity are a great gift that God has given to humankind. We live in a world where music can lift the soul, where stories can ignite the imagination.'[43]

Some expressions of Christianity have missed 'the Caedmon factor'. How would you describe what this is? What does it mean or might it mean for you?

Hilda was very senior and very busy, yet she made time to take seriously the gift of someone who perhaps had learning difficulties. She knew that 'the poetry is in the pity'.[44] Think about people who form the background to your life. Hold their potential before God.

Daring to throw away our false persona and listening to the dream of our heart, we may encounter the sun and the storm for the first time and find a glory in the ordinary.

In the night vision, Caedmon's soul sang out. Let us pray that the music of our souls may be unlocked:

Release, O Craftsperson of the universe:
The music of speech;
The music of thought;
The music of seeing.[45]

I cannot speak, unless you loose my tongue; I only stammer, and I speak uncertainly. But if you touch my mouth, my Lord, then I will sing the story of your wonders![46]

Struggle, praise and holy dying

What's in a name? Hilda's name meant 'struggle' or 'battle'. In 674, she contracted a horrible condition that racked her for the rest of her life. Its symptoms suggest that it might have been tuberculosis, a disease once known as consumption because of the severe weight loss it can cause. Its symptoms include coughing (often producing blood), fever, night sweats and chills. Hilda's final six years offered an unrivalled apprenticeship in the handling of suffering. Many might ask, 'Why should such a good person suffer such torture?' Bede, eulogising, suggested it was 'that her virtue might be made perfect in weakness' (see 2 Corinthians 12:9).

As the energy levels and available time of this redoubtable and energy-packed abbess declined, there were things she could no longer do. Yet, as her action in sending an advocate for Bosa's rights to Rome shows, she did not lose her focus. Bede tells us that during those six years of illness, Hilda 'never failed either to return thanks to her Maker, or publicly and privately to instruct the flock committed to her charge; for taught by her own experience she admonished all to serve the Lord dutifully, when health of body is granted to them, and always to return thanks faithfully to Him in adversity, or bodily infirmity'.

Hilda exemplified the pagan maxim that 'gratitude is the root of all virtue' and, even more, the apostle Paul's exhortation, 'Rejoice always, pray without ceasing, give thanks in all circumstances, for this is the will of God' (1 Thessalonians 5:16–17). More than a thousand years after Hilda's death, someone composed this 'Homily of Saint Hilda', which well captures her spirit:

> Trade with the gifts God has given you.
> Bend your minds to holy learning,
> that you may escape the fretting moth of littleness of mind
> that would wear out your souls.
> Brace your wills to actions that they may not be the spoils
> of weak desires.
> Train your hearts and lips to song which gives courage to the soul.
> Being buffeted by trials, learn to laugh.
> Being reproved, give thanks.
> Having failed, determine to succeed.

Despite her debilities, Hilda established a daughter monastery at Hackness for men and women, some 13 miles to the south of Whitby, in the last year of her life (680). In contrast to the bleak headland at Whitby, it was situated in a lush valley, and perhaps Hilda intended to spend her last days there, having appointed Frigyth as her resident deputy. Unlike other monasteries, which had separate cells, Hackness had a dormitory, and Bede's account is the first mention of a church bell in England. Tradition says that the monastery was built near the lake. If so, the site may have disappeared when the lake was enlarged in the 18th century. Hackness's present church of St Peter claims that its vestry was built in 1625 with stones from the original abbey. The *Anglo-Saxon Chronicle* records that the monastery was destroyed in 867 or 869 by the Danes Ingwe and Zubba. By 1066 it had vanished.

A woman called Begu was also at Hackness. If, as some believe, she was an Irish princess who escaped rape and found a safe haven in Northumbria, and whose vows were received by Bishop Aidan, it would not be surprising if she brought to the daughter monastery a 'seeing eye'.

In the seventh year of Hilda's sickness, the disease worsened, and her last days drew near. What thoughts passed through her mind as she lay dying? The traumas of her birth and fatherless infancy? The horrors of men devoured by battles and blaspheming, blood and boasting and killing? The story told to her childhood father-figure, Edwin, that likened a human life to a brief sparrow-flight through a lighted meeting hall, out of and into darkness? Hilda was now slipping into darkness. Did she recall the hook-nosed priest Paulinus who preached the gospel, instructed her and baptised her—or the books, especially the Gospels? The coming of Aidan—when Christ first walked out of the vellum pages of the Gospels into the byways of Northumbria, into the ways of its warriors and into her imagination and her heart's core? The deaths—Oswald and Aidan. The betrayals—Oswy. Despair beckoned her. 'Futility, futility,' says the Preacher in Ecclesiastes 1:2, 'all is futility.' What was it all for?

There were little Elfleda and her mother Enfleda—love overcoming all things. Yes, they had grown into love. There was the joy of being a spiritual mother to so many. Then there was that synod. So much was inevitable; so much was wrong. Her heart still retched at the loss of all those unforgettable Irish brothers at Lindisfarne. She had never seen or heard from them again. But then there was the monastery at Whitby and her students and the families, the tenants and the workers—Caedmon and the songs—these all passed through her heart. Yet (and again the abyss of despair threatened to engulf her), the pope had given Wilfrid his bishopric in her very own York. His boundaries were limited, certainly, but he had an unbounded determination that all the English should accede to his ways. His vision was vast but so imperious. Had her life been wasted? On and on, perhaps, inner demons and mixed memories passed through her.

In the darkness of her night, did she think about Caedmon who had found his calling in the night and had so recently died? Did she think of that nonchalant treasure she had brought to the attention of the English people, dying with a joke on his lips and a smile on his face? Did she think of Cuthbert, who watched over his sheep at night? She knew that he had been put in charge at Lindisfarne after the Irish had departed. She had often heard it told that, on the night Aidan died, Cuthbert had seen angels escorting Aidan into heaven. Did she think of Aidan, who went from heartbreak to heaven?

Did she think of Irish and Britons and Picts, of Romans and Anglo-Saxons, of royalty and Wilfrid and the royal souls who worked the earth, and the mothers? In death they were one, stripped of all that put them above or apart from others. Did she think about her name, Hilda, 'one who struggles', and about Jacob, who so struggled and overcame that he was renamed Israel? Would she herself be true to her name and her call to the very end?

Hilda chose. She chose to praise God to the last, to obey God to the last, and to give what God had given her to carry on behalf of the English people. God was all-giving, and she would be all-giving to the end. As the cock crowed, while it was still dark, she received Holy Communion and gave her final whispered words to her sisters and brothers who were gathered round: 'Preserve the peace of the gospel among yourselves, and also with *all* others.' While she was still speaking, she passed joyfully from death into life. She had given her all to her Maker, the Guardian of all. It was 17 November 680.

That same night, 13 miles away as the sisters slept in the dormitory at Hackness, Begu had an all-powerful vision. She heard the unforgettable sound of the bell they tolled when one of their sisters died. Its purpose was to wake them and call them to prayers in the chapel to accompany their deceased sister on her passage into heaven. She opened her eyes and thought she saw the monastery roof open, a heavenly light flooding the place with its bright beams. Looking earnestly at those beams of light, she saw the soul of Mother Hilda being carried to heaven, attended and guided by angels.

Begu, now fully awake and seeing everyone else still sleeping, realised that only she had heard and seen these things. In great fear, she ran to Abbess Frigyth and told her, with deep sobs and sighs, what she had seen. The abbess believed her and called all the sisters to the chapel, urging them to give themselves to prayer and the singing of psalms for the soul of their mother. This they did throughout the remainder of the night. At break of day, brothers from Whitby arrived with news of Hilda's death. The sisters informed them that they knew it already, and told how and when they had learned of it. Bede comments:

It appeared that her death had been revealed to them in a vision that same hour in which the brothers said that she had died. Thus by a fair harmony of events Heaven ordained, that when some saw her departure out of this world, the others should have knowledge of her entrance into the eternal life of souls. (Penguin, p. 214)

They would have had a funeral, of course. People from both highways and byways would have attended. We do not know what words they used, but we do know that more than a thousand years later, the eminent composer John Tavener composed the 'Ikon of Hilda' as part of his 1980 *Akhmatova: Requiem* and that churches use words such as the following 'Kontakion' in celebration of her life:

Blessed are you, mother of the Church,
radiant jewel lighting our darkness;
faithful in achievement and adversity;
disciple of Aidan; teacher of bishops; fosterer of nuns;
wise mentor, generous host;
friend of creation;
counsellor of rulers, patron of cowherds;
encourager of talents;
able teacher, noble in bearing;

105

constant in disappointment;
devoted to prayer, unceasing in praise.
Like a tree whose roots go deep, you bear the secret of growth and
the fruit of wisdom;
you seek to heal the wounded nations.
All glory to the Three of Tender love outpouring on you,
outpouring on us; one God, who mothers us all.[47]

Reflection

Hilda's spirituality celebrates Christ at the heart of life and offers praise in all our days.

If Christ is in you, though the body is dead because of sin, yet the spirit is alive because of righteousness.
ROMANS 8:10

From the time when Jacob wrestled with God, as if with a human partner, and eventually overcame, all Jewish people took their cue from and named themselves after this overcomer, 'Israel'. We have seen that Hilda's name, too, means 'one who struggles and overcomes'. The Jews' birthright, and ours, is to struggle and overcome.

Hilda suffered many pains: she suffered the pain of losing her father before her birth, and of losing her royal position and becoming a refugee when King Edwin was slain. If she married, she suffered the loss of her husband. She suffered the loss of the spiritual heritage of Aidan after the Synod of Whitby, and the pain of having to work with princes and prelates who played power games, and, for the last six years of her life, she suffered a debilitating disease.

Modern medicine has prolonged life and kept painful death at bay. Other forms of loss and pain have multiplied, however, owing to wars being brought into our living rooms through TV and the break-up of social relationships due to multiple choices and stress. We cannot even be sure that we shall remain immune to physical epidemics. *Time* magazine (4 March 2013) reported that strains of tuberculosis have emerged in India that are immune to all known TB drugs, and warned that a new Black Death could engulf humanity. So Hilda's way of living with pain and loss is of use to us.

The 'Dying Matters' movement reveals that over 70 per cent of us are uncomfortable about speaking of death. However, 'Death Cafés' are now multiplying, where ordinary people can discuss the subject over a scone and coffee. It can help if we visualise sufferings as birth pains, bringing Christ to birth as a seed that is buried gives birth to new shoots. What possibilities do you see?

Orthodox Christians refer to dying as 'the great passage' because it is a movement from one stage to another in a person's journey. It makes sense to practise leaving behind one stage of our journey and moving on to another throughout our lives. When we are dying, it may be helpful to look at a cross or ikon. I keep an ikon of Begu's vision of Hilda's death opposite my pillow.

In my book *Before We Say Goodbye*,[48] I have a liturgy of 'The voyage to the other side', in which the arriving soul says:

Now my dwelling is with God...
Neither pain nor sorrow are my lot...
But joy and light unfading...

Her friends on earth say:

Dear soul, weeping now is done.
Let our song rise with laughter,
Joy and praise to the Creator,
Alleluia. Alleluia. Amen

Wisdom and the role of women

Hilda has become an ikon of Wisdom—the rich nurturing and maternal dimension that is within God and which God has placed in the created order. Bede records that Aidan and his brothers loved Hilda heartily for her innate wisdom, that her prudence was such that she was consulted by many people from different walks of life and that all those who knew her called her 'mother'. Hilda had exceptional insight born of a mother's compassion.

This most capable spiritual mother reminds us of the capable wife described in the book of Proverbs, who 'rises while it is still night and provides food for her household and tasks for her servant girls. She considers a field and buys it; with the fruit of her hands she plants a vineyard. She girds herself with strength... She opens her hand to the poor... Strength and dignity are her clothing... She opens her mouth with wisdom... Many women have done excellently, but you surpass them all' (Proverbs 31:15–17, 20, 25–26, 29).

In general, Bede does not do justice to women. It is from Anglo-Saxon charters that we learn that a majority of monastic foundations were women's. Even in Kent, eleven out of 22 charters until AD760 were for women's foundations. Not a few, like Hilda's, were double monasteries for men and women, led by an abbess. Britain has never seen the like before or since, and nor (with two exceptions) have other parts of Christendom. Archbishop Theodore boggled at this. His Penitential decreed that 'it is not allowed for [communities of] men to have female monks, nor [those of women] men; but let us not destroy that which is the custom in this country.'

To explain the unparalleled role of Hilda and her like, we need to look at the revival of Christian community in the woman-friendly Irish style that was familiar to Aidan and was brought by Columbanus to Frankia; we can also note that a similar development took place more than a century later in the German church. There, 36 new communities for noblewomen were founded between 919 and 1024 in one diocese alone. In all three regions, England, Frankia and Germany, these developments were part of the flush of enthusiasm of new converts from paganism.

Professor Conrad Leyser, Lecturer in Medieval History at Oxford University, in a study of Anglo-Saxon monasteries, thought that these parallel developments prompted the question 'whether there was not some underlying predicament in the pre-Christian beliefs and make-up of Franks, Saxons and Anglo-Saxons to which the endowment of nunneries furnished a welcome and eagerly sought after solution'.[49] Men were the warrior invaders who seized lands, properties and women. If, as often happened, they were killed in battle, their women and children were left to fend for themselves. So the creation of stable centres of livelihood, learning and prayerfulness, where each person was treated with respect, was enormously attractive to women: it was a form of women's liberation.

Christine Fell points out that we can deduce from Aldhelm's late seventh-century letters (for example, to the nuns of Barking) the wide range of these nuns' scholarly activities. Aldhelm speaks of their remarkable mental disposition, 'roaming widely through the flowering fields of scripture... now scrutinising with careful application the hidden mysteries of the ancient laws... Now exploring wisely the fourfold text (of the Gospels)... now duly rummaging through the old stories of the historians and the entries of chroniclers... now sagaciously inquiring into the rules of the grammarians and the teachers of experts on... the rules of metrics.'[50] There is no reason to suppose that Whitby nuns were much different.

Later royal abbesses turned their monasteries into courts. Hilda certainly received many members of royalty, while Enfleda had Oswy and, later, the remains of her father King Edwin buried at Whitby: it became the royal burial ground. Hilda, however, never removed her village from ordinary life. She made no distinction between a peasant and a prince, a prelate and a novice; she had space in her heart for each, believed in each and loved each. That is why uneducated people and royals alike called her mother, as also did 'foreigners' from outside her own kingdom of Deira.

As we have seen already, Hilda was succeeded as abbess by the widowed queen Enfleda, and then by her daughter Elfleda. Both were declared saints in their own right. Reading between the lines of Bede's sparse description of Hilda, we cannot but conclude that she exercised an extraordinary leadership role. Bede notes that Hilda's successor as abbess was assisted by Bishop Trumwine, which is perhaps a hint that Enfleda was unable to manage all Hilda's responsibilities on her own. More important than Hilda's great energy and ability, however, was her management style of love.

The double community at Whitby came to a sudden end in 867 when the Vikings invaded the area, and the monastery remained in ruins until after the Norman Conquest. It would be wrong to assume, however, that the hinterland of the 'village of God' was uniformly destroyed. The 'Memorial of Benefactions', which is the oldest entry in the Whitby Register, or Abbot's Book, suggests that the district around the monastery was one of the busiest scenes of Danish colonisation.

When the Normans colonised England in 1066, they imposed a feudal, male-dominated society even in the church, and belittled women. Not for a thousand years would a woman again be allowed to lead as had Hilda. Even so, the Normans eventually built a new abbey near the site of Hilda's monastery and dedicated it to both St Peter and St Hilda.

Men have written the Bible and the church's liturgies and have controlled clerical hierarchy down the centuries. Men have made out that God was in *their* image, yet a theology that claims that God is male has always been a Christian heresy. It has always been mainstream Christian theology that God created humans male and female and that this polarity reflects something of God's likeness (Genesis 1:27).

In recent generations, the rise of feminism and greater openness to the Spirit have revolutionised the role of women. In the 1980s, the World Council of Churches held consultations on the search for a 'more complete and authentic community of women and men'. In a Faith and Order study document, *Church and World: the Unity of the Church and the Renewal of Human Community* (1990), it was stated:

A true community of women and men is God's gift and promise for humanity, which is created 'in God's image'—male and female (Gen. 1:27); and the church, as prophetic sign of that which God desires for women and men, is called to embody that community in its own life…

The domination of women by men does not belong to human community as intended in God's creation (Gen. 2:23) but to the consequences of sin, which distort the community of women and men as well as the relationship between human beings and nature (Gen. 3:16–19).

The Community of Women and Men in the Church, which became part of Churches Together in Britain and Ireland in 1981, used this prayer by Janet Morley:

*God our vision, in our mother's womb
you formed us for your glory.*

As your servant Hilda
shone like a jewel in the Church,
may we now delight
to claim her gifts of wisdom and nurturing
reflected in the women of this age.
COPYRIGHT © JANET MORLEY

I met with the Community of Women and Men in the Church at Ushaw College, County Durham, for a weekend on 'Abbess Hilda—Christ's "Jewel in the Darkness" and a Mother of the Church in Britain', led by representatives of the Roman Catholic, Russian Orthodox and Anglican Churches and the Quakers. At the meeting, John Arnold, the Dean of Durham, explained that for 900 years women had been physically excluded from the main part of the church, but the cathedral had recently 'invited women back', installing an ikon of Mary in one chapel and an ikon of Saint Hilda, by Edith Reytiens, in the Galilee Chapel.

In the 1980s, the Movement for the Ordination of Women (MOW) became active among most Protestant churches, as did the Catholic Women's Network. There were many offshoots, including St Hilda's Community, formed in 1987 as a worshipping community open to experiment in liturgy and to the ministry of women. Certain traditionalists argued that, since Hilda was never ordained, these people were confusing ordination with leadership. As if to rub in this point, two decades later a few Anglicans opposed to women bishops, most of whom were also opposed to women priests, set up the Society of St Wilfrid and St Hilda, which campaigned to have separate jurisdictions for traditionalists with this view.

Lesley McLean of MOW Australia conducted an online quiet day in 2012, entitled 'Learning, gentleness and the arts: Abbesses of Saxon England as models of ministry'. She teaches:

The Anglo-Saxons integrated worship and study with delight in the beauty of holiness. They took seriously the notion of gifts as from God so that their artistic gifts glorified the Gospel. Words mattered, so their monks and nuns illuminated manuscripts, and their monasteries had magnificent books in church for anyone to read at any time... They sang their prayers. Singing mattered: they were a singing people... It seems to me Hilda never lost that Christian ideal that what we do for the least of these we do it for Jesus. This is gentleness born of humility, a word derived from the Latin for 'earth'. Hilda's model of ministry is gentle because it is based on the common humanity we share that is formed in the image and likeness of God. Gentleness cares, is attentive, has no bias. It is authority that comes from the author of peace and lover of concord.[51]

In art, Hilda and other abbesses are depicted holding a crozier, which is a bishop's sign of authority. On the day in 2012 when the Church of England General Synod voted at first not to ordain women as bishops, the vicar of St Hilda's Church in Hartlepool, Christopher Collison, signed off an email to me: 'From St Hilda's Church, where midweek services are held under the gaze of a woman holding a crozier'.

Reflection

Wisdom is a many-splendoured treasure: it ranges from everyday common sense to an eternal aspect of the divine. In English, the word 'wisdom' has two roots—the Latin *wis*, meaning 'vision', and the Old English *dom*, referring to judgment. One Wisdom book in the Apocrypha speaks of her thus:

As a mother shall she meet him.
With the Bread of Understanding
shall she feed him,
and give him the Water of Wisdom to drink. (Ben Sirach 15:2–3)

In the second millennium, Western Christianity as a whole became male-dominated, but Celtic Christians held on to the insight revealed in the traditional saying 'There's a mother's heart in the heart of God'.

Such insights can, of course, be found in the Bible, with mother birds used to describe God. We find references to a mother hen (Luke 13:34), a mother eagle (Deuteronomy 32:11) and the dove of the Spirit (Genesis 1:2), who broods over chaos to bring creation to birth. 'Stork' in Hebrew is *hasida*, which translates as 'tender mother' from its observed habit of staying with its young to the point of death. It is the same word as *hesed*, which means loving faithfulness, the word that describes God.

The Lord says, 'Can a woman forget her nursing-child or show no compassion for the child of her womb? Even these may forget, yet I will not forget you' (Isaiah 49:15). We also read, in another Wisdom book, 'When you stand among your elders, decide who is wise and join them... If you discover a wise person, rise early to visit them' (Wisdom 6:32, 36). Many people visited Hilda, and many think the time has come to revisit her. I have invited members of various retreats to intuit the characteristics they associate with Hilda. As a result I have compiled the following list:

- Having a big enough heart without being anyone's fool.
- Enabling much to come to birth, without allowing that which has already come to birth to die out through lack of a secure, affirming framework in which to grow.
- Maintaining consistency; standing with the marginalised without losing our own identity.

A group of women meeting in Harare, Zimbabwe, wanted to grow in maturity and have a safe place to come and learn more about how to do so. It seemed that each woman had the calling of 'spiritual mothering' on her, and each became a nucleus of growth and stability in her own home and the parts of society in which she worked. They aimed to follow Hilda's example of helping her nuns to 'follow their rule', as well as helping people to find their callings (as she did for Caedmon) and providing opportunities for them to grow in those callings.

A group with prophetic gifting who visited the women spoke of Zimbabwe as a nation of spiritual orphans, asking where the spiritual mothers and fathers were. They gained an increased impetus to seek ways in which the Holy Spirit is opening up new channels for this gift of spiritual mothering to be identified and developed in a new generation of women.

The fruits of Hilda's life and ministry may be linked with the fruit of the Holy Spirit (Galatians 5:22–23). Meditate upon these verses in the light of what you have learned about Hilda. Which of the reports from contemporary foundations dedicated to St Hilda speaks to you most? What other fruits of Hilda's life do you see or envisage? In what ways are you being inspired by these examples?

The fruits of Hilda continue in those who, like her:

- find their end in their beginning with God.
- redeem the time during their hidden years.
- say 'Yes!' at their midlife crossroads.
- establish community and soul-friendship.
- reconcile fratricidal parties.
- release the power of possibility.

Along with the Zimbabweans:

We pray for a recovery of spiritual motherhood that will:
instil a confidence in Christ that energises and frees the other to leave childish attachments and face the world with love;

allow healing to come through patience and sensitive listening.

enable creativity to be born and talent to blossom.

kindle the desire for holy living.

accept that we are incomplete and bear one another's pain.

embrace and reconcile those of clashing views.

teach us to drink deeply from the wells of wisdom.

model for us ordered lives, sustaining relationships and lifelong learning.

inspire in us the practice of reflection and the habit of praise.

grow the church to maturity.

become a channel of life, blessing and direction for others.

nurture a nation and shape it for God.[52]

Which particular aspects of 'spiritual mothering' (or fathering) do you feel drawn to? Place them in order of importance. Dialogue with the Lord about why you have these motivations and what he is saying to you through them, and develop a plan of action (like a growth plan) to which you intend to be faithful.

Fruits, vampires and victory

In Jesus' time, official religious leaders thought that he had no part in 'the true religion' as defined by its outward hierarchy, rituals and rules. In Hilda's time, a similar danger threatened the church. Those who sought to live the simple humanity of Jesus, some of them inspired by the departed Irish, perhaps felt they had no part in the games that the legalist Romanisers played in the new empire of Christendom. Hilda, however, played her part with integrity and with great effect. She embraced the struggle between external and internal desire. People of different points of view related to her as a spiritual mother.

A task awaits Hilda's spiritual children—to nurture a new generation, release the music in every heart, and transform dark passions into sacrificial love and ghost towns into villages of God. In this final chapter we shall explore how far-reaching are Hilda's fruits; how, in Whitby itself, she has been overshadowed by the legend of Dracula, and how a contemporary rediscovery of her spirituality can usher in something more lasting and life-giving than the dark forces—a priceless treasure available to all who search until they find.

By the time Hilda died, Christianity was no longer about a lone bishop travelling around. It had a significant number of powerful heartlands where prayer and work, study, art and mission flourished. Hilda's heartland sent out many God-inspired workers, and its library housed the writings of significant theologians, such as Jerome, whose descriptions of the desert 'athletes of Christ', who conquered the demons, inspired the English as much as they had the Irish. The works of Aldhelm were probably there also, since the one letter we have of Elfleda's suggests his influence.

Hilda was celebrated in the eighth-century Calendar of St Willibrord and the ninth-century *Liber Vitae Ecclesiae Dunelmensis*, which was probably compiled at Lindisfarne.[53] There are indications in *The Old English Martyrology*, a collection of over 230 hagiographies, probably compiled in Mercia in the second half of the ninth century, that its compiler knew of a *Life* of Hilda, although that is now lost. The York missal celebrates Hilda's 'translation'—that is, her elevation into a shrine—on 25 August.

The twelfth-century chronicler William of Malmesbury records that after the Danes destroyed the Whitby monastery, Hilda's relics, along with those of many Northumbrian saints, were brought to Glastonbury. The various transcriptions of his account diverge greatly. In one text, the movement of the relics took place in the tenth century; in another, the relics were taken by Northumbria's Abbot Tica, who was appointed Abbot of Glastonbury in 754. The wording of a separate entry in William of Malmesbury's *The History of English Kings* supports this earlier date, but, since the Vikings did not ravage Lindisfarne until 793, questions must remain. The Glastonbury tradition of an Abbot Tica (variously spelt) who fled south with Hilda's bones is also found in a Glastonbury commonplace book of the 15th and 16th centuries. A 14th-century Latin *Life of The Holy Abbess Hilda*, from the abbey at Romsey, is almost entirely based upon Bede. In a *Life of Saint Hilda* which is now lost but which John Lelan inspected at Whitby in the 16th century, it says that 'Titus, the Abbot, escaped to Glastonbury with the relics of St Hilda'. Hilda's name appears in four post-1100 Benedictine calendars from Durham, Chester, Evesham and Westminster.

The Bodleian Library in Oxford has a 14th-century manuscript (Rawlinson Liturgy B.1) known as the Whitby Missal because it gives prominence to Saints Hilda and Begu. These shreds of legacy cannot hide the fact that the Viking invasions and then the Norman conquest obliterated Aidan's and Hilda's communities and caused their heritage to be neglected for a thousand years.

However, in the ever-changing collective unconscious, not only of Britain and Ireland but later of the English-speaking world and then of the entire global village, a yearning for a new yet old archetypal dimension was stirring, which Hilda embodied.

With the development of education for women in the late 19th century, schools and colleges in many lands were dedicated to Hilda. Numerous Anglican, Roman Catholic and other churches bear her name, as do several movements and new communities.

St Hilda's College, Oxford, was founded in 1893 as a hall for women, and became co-educational in 2006. Princess Haya, an alumna of St Hilda's College, was the first Arab and first woman to serve as Goodwill Ambassador for the United Nations World Food Programme (from 2005 to 2007) and to compete in equestrian sports at Olympic level.

St Hilda's & St Hugh's School in Chengalpattu, India, serves 530 children. It was founded after the devastation of the 2004 tsunami, when the Church of South India identified an area that would most benefit from resources offered by St Hilda's and St Hugh's School in New York. Each summer, members of its faculty spend time with its twin school in India, working with staff and teaching its students. A continuing bond has been forged between them. The Chengalpattu school now serves southern India's most disadvantaged caste, the Dalits, giving children who would not otherwise have access to education the chance to learn, succeed and change their futures. The aims of St Hilda's & St Hugh's School, New York, are to encourage a respect for nature and human achievement and a love for art, music, drama and athletics, and to ensure that each member of the school is cherished and invited to grow in knowledge, faith, and love of self and others.

The Community of Sisters of the Church opened a school in Liverpool, UK, fired up by the philosophy of their founder that children should first be taught to know the love of God. This was later named St Hilda's School and was placed under the care of the Church of England Diocese of Liverpool. Today it is a teeming anthill of activity with a widely acknowledged reputation for excellence.

There are also schools dedicated to St Hilda in Singapore, Western Australia, New Zealand and Canada.

St Hild's School, Hartlepool Headland, held an event to celebrate local community initiatives, which they named 'Hilda's Jewels'. They then launched the 2014 Year of Hilda by producing an educational game named 'Hild's Jewels'.

Churches dedicated to Hilda are too numerous to count. St Hilda's, Gezina, is part of the Anglican Church of Southern Africa. Its ethos is well expressed by its Archbishop, Thabo Makgoba: 'We find our humanity through the humanity of others—we flourish through promoting the flourishing of others.'

Hilda has inspired new forms of community. In 1858, a Society of St Peter was formed at Horbury, near Wakefield, which lies within the area of ancient Northumbria; it was dedicated to help women who had succumbed to the appalling poverty and crime of the congested mill towns. It founded a St Hilda's School for girls, followed by two more schools, in Lancashire and the Bahamas. Margaret Cope became Head of School and, three years later, at the age of 25, she became a postulant. There were difficulties in the Society, and, with the outbreak of World War I, the school closed. When news of this reached two teachers who were on holiday at Goathland, near Whitby, they sent details of properties that might be suitable for a school in Whitby. Margaret Cope, known as Sister Sylvia (her middle name), purchased Sneaton Castle, secured release from her vows and moved, with several sisters and secular teachers, from St Hilda's School at Horbury to St Hilda's School in Whitby.

By 1917, the Archbishop of York had permitted Sister Sylvia to found a new Order of the Holy Paraclete. The school was extended, a St Hilda's Priory was built and a farm acquired. Over the ensuing century, branch houses in England were established, as well as houses and schools in Africa. Ecumenical and reconciliation links with Sweden, Scotland and Northern Ireland have developed, while Sneaton Castle was transformed from a school into a conference centre in 1997.

The sisters describe themselves as an Order rooted and grounded in love, dedicated to God's Holy Spirit, whose ideal is a balanced life of prayer, work and recreation in which every activity is regarded as a sacrament. They own a sizeable area of land at Whitby, which includes shop, farm, conference centre and priory. Now they offer a welcome to 'along-siders'—people who do not make monastic vows but share the vision and desire to live alongside the community. If enough entrepreneurial Christians were to come, who knows whether there might again be a bustling village of God there?[54]

In the 1990s, a dispersed ecumenical community emerged, which named itself the Community of Aidan and Hilda. It seeks to offer fresh expressions of Hilda's principles: a holistic Rule or Way of Life, lifelong learning, churches as villages of God, and culture-friendly mission that unlocks the poetry in the shyest person. It describes its life-giving principles as: '

Simplicity—that we may experience more of the generosity of God.
Purity—that we may experience more of the love of God.
Obedience—that we may experience more of the freedom of God.

Each member renews their vows on St Hilda's Day, 17 November, pledging 'to follow a daily rhythm of prayer, work and re-creation, to meet with their Soul Friend, to make an annual retreat… and to follow the example of Aidan, Hilda and kindred saints.'

In Whitby itself, however, all is not well. It began in the 1890s, when Bram Stoker wrote a fictional novel about Count Dracula, a vampire who arrives in Britain from Transylvania, having been shipwrecked at Whitby. It became a cult novel and, since then, more than 200 films have been made that feature Dracula, and endless new versions of his story continue to be printed. These have spawned an extraordinary vampire subculture, which has blinded people to the real birthright of Whitby. At times the town is overrun by Dracula fantasists who search for his grave in the churchyard opposite the site of Hilda's abbey, or by Goths who hold regular weekend gatherings there. Local traders fill their shops with items that appeal to these cult visitors, and a 'Dracula Experience' has been marketed.

When Bram Stoker took a holiday in Whitby in 1890, he was, by all accounts, quite smitten with the town, the abbey and the church with its tombstones. He borrowed a book from Whitby library entitled *An Account of the Principalities of Wallachia and Moldavia* (1820) by William Wilkinson, and made notes from it, including the observation that Dracula, in the Wallachian language, means 'Devil'. Stoker decided to change the name of his vampire Count from Wampyr to Dracula.

Most of Stoker's sources, in fact, came from elsewhere, and Whitby is only a minor backdrop in his story. Dracula is on his way to London on the Russian schooner, Demeter; it is only because he is shipwrecked near Whitby that he comes ashore in the guise of a black dog and wreaks havoc on the town. One character, named Mina, keeps a journal containing detailed descriptions of Whitby and those areas frequented by Dracula: 'Right over the town is the ruin of Whitby Abbey, which was sacked by the Danes, and which is the scene of part of "Marmion", where the girl was built up in the wall. It is a most noble ruin, of immense size, and full of beautiful and romantic bits; there is a legend that a white lady is seen in one of the windows.' It is surely time to introduce Dracula readers to the real white lady behind the abbey.

Although the attraction of the Dracula genre is the horror of sucking blood from people until they die, Stoker does briefly identify in his novel two things that might be more powerful than the bloodsucker—a wafer from a Eucharist (because it makes present Christ's blood, which saves the world), and a crucifix that brings home to people the cross on which Christ bled to death before rising again.

Dracula fans seem unaware of any connection between their vampire stories and Hilda's monastery site upon the hill, but there is a connection. The *Life of Gregory* written at the Whitby monastery around 680–704 includes legends of two excommunicated nuns who died but were then seen in the church. After St Benedict sent some consecrated bread to their former nurse in order that it might be offered for their reconciliation, they always remained quietly in their graves. Gregory also related the story of a dead and buried Benedictine priest whose body was found above ground. A consecrated wafer was placed on his breast, and his body was reinterred and remained there in peace. Such tales were made popular in the mid-1700s by a Benedictine monk, Dom Augustin Calmet, whose stories most probably stand behind Bram Stoker's use of the eucharistic wafer and the crucifix as weapons against vampires.

There are two sides to every story. The time is surely ripe for the 'Hilda' side of the Whitby story to come into its own. Dracula represents an undiluted evil force that threatens to overwhelm and envelop the whole persona. To combat this negative force, the story's author has created a band of good and brave men, but they lack the power of Dracula. In Stoker's novel, the crucifix does play a major role in each of the climaxes, where the vampires Lucy and Dracula are killed, but Stoker only scratches at its edge. The evil cower at the sight of it, for it represents God and all that is good and pure. The Devil hates what it represents so tries to remove all signs of it. After Lucy dies, the doctor Van Helsing places 'a small golden crucifix over her mouth' in an attempt to save her soul. When she turns into a vampire, the crucifix is, again, one of the weapons that the men use. Nevertheless, the lasting impression of the novel is the stench of evil and the ineffectiveness of the forces of good.

The other side of the story might begin with Hilda's name, which indicates that she is a supreme battler who overcomes all manner of evils. The elements of her mother Breguswith's name are *brego* ('king' or 'chief') and *swith* ('strong, mighty'). Hilda's sister's name, Hereswith, means 'battle', and it seems that Hilda's full name was actually Hildeswith or something similar (also meaning 'battle strong')—the last element of the name being passed down through the family.[55]

The other side of the story might continue with two legends about the 'white lady in the abbey'. Legends are not quite the same as history, but they tell us something of the impression a person makes on others. The first legend has it that, as the birds fly past the high headland abbey, they lower their wings as if saluting the spiritual authority of Mother Hilda that lingers there still. The birds in the original story were wild geese; a later historian (Lionel Charlton) changed the geese into seagulls since, by his time, the wide marshy estuary that attracted the weary wildfowl had been changed by human reclamation. Whatever the changes, as humans lift their hands in worship, so perhaps birds lower their wings—in recognition of a unique spiritual presence.

Among the Gothic paraphernalia in Whitby shops, a visitor might also find a piece of ammonite for sale. Ammonite could once be found on Whitby's shore, although little is now left. The second legend is that the ammonites are the petrified remains of snakes that once infested the area. The infestation was brought to an end by Hilda, who turned the snakes into stone in order to clear a site for the building of an abbey. Her actions are immortalised in Sir Walter Scott's poem 'Marmion' (1808):

When Whitby's nuns exalting told
Of thousand snakes, each one
Was changed into a coil of stone,

When Holy Hilda pray'd:
Themselves, without their holy ground,
Their stony folds had often found.

Snakes symbolise evil. People thought that the effect of Hilda's presence was to leave evil curled up in a powerless petrified lump at her feet. Hilda was light and Hilda was victory: that is what the legends say.[56]

The legends are but the appetisers to the alternative, utterly real narrative. This tells us that, in Hilda's life and death, we discover goodness to be stronger than evil, love stronger than hatred, and Christ's life-blood stronger than death.

The Irish who so inspired Hilda linked this glorious truth with the idea that each believer has their place of resurrection. Irish Christians thought it was important to be buried in the place God had called them to be, so that at the general resurrection they would be best placed to continue their work in a transformed earth. Bede describes Herbert, the Derwentwater hermit, requesting his soul friend Cuthbert that they might each go to their place of resurrection on the same day—which they did.

The New Testament scholar N.T. Wright, a former Bishop of Durham, reminds us that heaven is not a mere dream of an afterlife, designed to make the thought of dying less awful; it is God's space, while earth is our space. The two overlap and, in the general resurrection, when there is a renewed heaven and earth, the two become one. In the light of Hilda's angel-lit passage to heaven, we may conclude that Whitby is her place of resurrection.

In Hilda's place of resurrection, Goths can discover, as they have done in other places, that 'Golgotha' (the name of the site of Christ's original cross) can become 'Goth church'. A survey of the Cambridge Goth community suggested that anything up to a third of 'Goths' considered themselves to be in some sense Christian. One journalist put it like this when discussing St Edward's Cambridge and its Goth Eucharist:

Church services are all about a misunderstood man who got nailed to a cross. They are held in a looming, bell-towered, candle-lit edifice in the middle of a graveyard. Indeed, if you go catholic, you get to burn incense and drink blood, as well. By contrast, playing a bit of Rasmus looks a bit, well, townie.[57]

Many young people know more about vampires and 'twilight' films than they do about Jesus, but the evils that Jesus alone can overcome are more than myths of vampires. Our world is being drained by money sharks, phone hackers, media character assassins and greedy consumers.

A hopeful sign is that pilgrims are on the increase in Hilda's place of resurrection, as elsewhere. Local Christians have produced a pilgrim trail leaflet in the steps of St Hilda, from the well named after her on the beach, up the 199 steps to the St Caedmon cross in the graveyard, or up the winding Caedmon's Trod to the abbey, there to pause in the presence of God.

Sometimes, in my mind's eye, I see Goths and pilgrims intermingling. They climb the steps up to the graveyard, some vainly imagining or pretending that Dracula or other people of the dark are buried there, but between the top step and the graves stands a high stone cross. St Caedmon's cross was unveiled in 1898 by Britain's then Poet Laureate, Alfred Austin. The cross is 20 feet high and hewn out of fine-grained hard sandstone. Upon its front are carved panels of Christ in the act of blessing, King David playing his harp, Abbess Hilda, and Caedmon in the stable, inspired to sing his great song. On the arms of the cross above are the symbols of the four Gospel writers. Below is the inscription: 'To the glory of God and in memory of His servant Caedmon... and the Lamb of God (Agnus Dei)'. On the reverse side is carved a double vine, symbolic of Christ and his fruits in his people; in the loops are portrayed four of Hilda's most fruitful apprentices—Bosa, Aetla, Oftfor and John of Beverley.

I imagine that the tree of the cross speaks again: 'God so loved the world that he gave his only Son, that everyone who believes in him may not perish but may have eternal life' (John 3:16). They kneel before the cross. Others join them—Hilda's aspiring spiritual children. No longer do they wish to fritter away their time with life-drainers and graves of the dark. They want to spend time with the young Warrior, the Son of God, and with Hilda, his heroic struggler against every dark force that seeks to divide, debilitate or destroy. Some newly arrived Whitby residents join them. Inspired by Pope Francis' challenge that the church might become 'the home of all, not a small chapel that holds a small group of selected people',[58] they have a passion to restore Whitby as a village of God.

They enter the church and offer prayers that Hilda's spiritual children will transform dark forces into places of resurrection:

> In the hard places we will rise up with visions from on high.
> In times of exile and loss we will take hope
> from the witnesses God sends.
> In the place of success we will descend into the sacrificial ways
> of the Servant Christ.
> In the unexpected encounters we will open ourselves
> to the warmth of human love.
> In our disagreements we will weave God's overarching tapestry.
> In our recreation we will release the song in every human heart.
> In our sickness and dying we will deploy the weapons of praise
> until the kingdoms of this world become the kingdom of our God.

Other pilgrims wend their way up Caedmon's Trod. They sing songs of faith. Songs that were locked up deep in the souls of vampire hunters are now released. Like a symphony they all find themselves singing:

> Blessed Hilda, holy mother,
> friend of Aidan, Christ's own stalk;
> born to honour—stripped of father,

finding faith, baptised at York;
shining as a radiant jewel,
lighting up our darkened walk.

Taught of God by Wearside river,
daring, learning, steeped in prayer;
you became a guide to many,
friend of people far and near;
drawing out the cowherd's talents,
held by earth and heav'n most dear.

Faithful host and reconciler,
staying true through shifting ties;
thankful in success and trial,
always fair and always wise;
meditater, motivator,
wisdom's gem, and heaven's prize,

Mother of a myriad children
Wisdom's ikon, paradigm—
Spill your seed into new peoples
Souls from every realm and clime
Songs releasing, poems making,
Pains embracing, with us shine.

Barely noticed, away from the noise of the crowds, a few thoughtful people make their way to the empty field that adjoins the site of Hilda's ancient monastery. These people are silent. They stop. They become still. A voice as quiet as a wind's whisper and as gentle as gossamer says, 'The kingdom of heaven is like treasure hidden in a field, which someone found and hid; then in his joy he goes and sells all that he has and buys that field' (Matthew 13:44).

This book is the story of a jewel from that treasure.

Appendix

St Hilda pilgrimage routes

York Minster

In the eastern crypt of the Minster is sited a font, under which was a well, the place where, traditionally, Hilda along with King Edwin and many others was baptised in 627.

Whitby

The Abbey can be approached from the town by walking up the 199 church steps or by car from the main road bridge to the south side of the river. The Abbey is cared for by English Heritage. In the town, Whitby Museum in Pannet Park has artefacts from Hilda's time and later. One of the most interesting is a seventh-century comb.

A St Hilda meditation trail

A leaflet with suggestions for a meditative walk in the steps of St Hilda has been produced by local people, with these stopping places, together with suggested activities for each place:

- The Healing Spring (when the tide is out) at the foot of the cliff lift on West Cliff. This comes out on to the beach next to the spa. Pray for healings.

- The caves. Walk along the beach towards the pier when the tide is out and see caves where early Christians may have prayed. Make a cross from driftwood.
- The pier. Walk to the lighthouse and read the plaque on the old lighthouse. St Hilda possibly arrived in Whitby at this spot. Reflect upon mission journeys.
- The Fish Quays. Walk towards the bridge over the River Esk, past the fish quays and amusements. Goths and Dracula devotees may be in evidence. Think about Christ's call to fish for people and to transform them.
- Caedmon's Trod. Cross the bridge over the river and walk up Bridge Street, then follow the right-hand bend around to the right. On your left is a signpost to Caedmon's Trod and the Abbey Walk, between the buildings opposite the Friends Meeting House. Think about our journey towards God and the song in every human heart waiting to be unlocked. Pray about this for people you know.
- Caedmon's cross. At the top, walk along Aelfeda's Terrace towards the church, and pray inside. Leave the church by the top gate, turn left to the Caedmon cross at the top of the 199 steps. Reflect on King David and Caedmon and their harps, and sing praises to God, either in your heart or aloud. Walk across the grass to the cliff edge that overlooks the sea and town below. This is thought to be the site of Hilda's original monastery. Linger here, reimagining her life, her thoughts, and a typical day in Hilda's monastery—a village of God, in which everyone had a part.

St Hilda's Priory Chapel, Sneaton Castle, is open daily from 09.00 to 11.30 and 14.00 to 16.00. The site shop is open from 13.30 to 16.30, Mondays to Saturdays.

Lilla's Cross

On the lonely moor track between Whitney and Hackness is a seventh-century stone sentinel cross dedicated to Lilla, the thegn who saved the life of Hilda's uncle, King Edwin, at the cost of his own. It was possibly named by Hilda. It is by far the oldest Christian monument, and probably the finest on the North York Moors. It is situated only about a mile north-east of the Fylingdales Early Warning Radar Station on Lilla Rigg. The Bronze Age round barrow, which allegedly contained his remains and on which the cross stands, is known as Lilla Howe.

Hackness

From Whitby take the A171 Scarborough road, turning right through Harwood Dale to Hackness. In Hackness church there are preserved fragments of an Anglian stone cross from the monastery that Hilda founded, probably from the early part of the eighth century.

Ellerburn

From Hackness take the road through the beautiful Forge Valley to the main Pickering road, the A170. Tradition says that there was a preaching station here in Hilda's time. Ellerburn would have served the students from Hilda's monastery as a midway base for their missionary outreach into pagan villages. The eleventh-century church has pieces of eighth- and ninth-century Saxon crosses built into the walls: these are indicated in an excellent guidebook.

Danby

St Hilda's Church, Danby, lies at the heart of Danby Dale, some two miles from the centre of the village. It is on a very ancient site and incorporates Saxon and Norman remains. Hilda is depicted in the 'missionary window'.

Hinderwell

The church of St Hilda at Hinderwell, which derives its name from Hilda's Holy Well, has a spring of pure water located in the churchyard on the north side of the church. One legend says that Hilda had a retreat cell here, another that she stopped off here on a journey when she was tired and thirsty, and, through prayer, discovered this source of water.

Loftus

Another potentially early site is Three Crosses Well at Loftus.

Hartlepool

During excavations connected with house-building in 1833, the cemetery of Hilda's monastery was discovered, some 150 yards south-east of the present St Hilda's Church, which stands like a beacon on the Hartlepool headland, a mile or two from the present town centre.

In following years, several named gravestones were discovered. Four are preserved in London's British Museum, two in the Museum of Antiquities at Newcastle-upon-Tyne, one in the library at Durham Cathedral and one at St Hilda's Church in Hartlepool. The stone in the church bears an inscription to a female named Hildithryth, which has led some to speculate that it may refer to St Hilda. Other scholars have thought that one of the British Museum's graveyard stones is that of Hilda's mother, Breguswith (although this view is not supported by the Museum).

No trace of the Hartlepool monastery remains today, but Hartlepool Museum has a reconstruction of Hilda's monasteries, showing the separate enclosures for women and men, ploughed fields, animal enclosures, graveyard and workers' huts in the fishing village. Hartlepool Abbey was featured in a March 2000 episode of the British TV programme *Time Team* (Channel 4) called 'Nuns in Northumbria', in which bones and a book clasp were found. A name stone found during the cemetery excavations is on display in St Hilda's Church.

St Hilda's Church has a visitor centre, charting the history of the church and the headland, with modern displays (some interactive) and welcomers on hand to guide you round and tell you more. It states, 'In keeping with our monastic origins, and as a member of the Open Churches Trust, St Hilda's welcomes visitors both to services and on Saturdays from 2 to 4 pm throughout the year and also on Wednesdays and Sundays, from 2 to 4 pm, from Easter to September. Refreshments are available.'

In front of St Hilda's Church, local authorities have created a square where a Celtic cross has been laid before an ancient cross base. A plaque states: 'This 21st-century cross has been erected to celebrate the Christian heritage of Hartlepool since 640AD. The steps are from the original pilgrims cross which once stood on the route from Lindisfarne (Holy Island) to Hartlepool.'

Cumbria and beyond

During the Norman period, a church dedicated to Hilda had a 'Hermitage of Holy Hild in the Forest of Englewood'. The spelling, Hildekirk, is concealed in the current name, Islekirk Hall.

The delight of being a pilgrim scholar might be to journey to Carlisle, then across the border from Hadrian's Wall to Bewcastle and Ruthwell to see the ancient monuments there, and then to Vercelli in Italy to see its manuscript. The elements comprising the Ruthwell cross and that at Bewcastle, as well as the famous poem in runes sculpted upon Ruthwell, seem to come from all the cultural elements present at Iona, Whitby, Lindisfarne and

Jarrow. They are a glorious mixture of Irish, Anglo-Saxon and Byzantine styles, a truly cosmopolitan gathering.

A St Hilda pilgrimage by boat from Lindisfarne to Whitby

- Lindisfarne: Visit St Mary's Church and churchyard, the probable site of the Celtic monastery that Hilda may have visited. Also see the chapel of the Open Gate, the Retreat House of the Community of Aidan and Hilda, which has ikons and liturgies of St Hilda.
- Bamburgh: Visit the castle and church where Aidan died. Hilda may have met with Aidan in these places.
- Warkworth: Moor the boat in the harbour at the river mouth. Visit St Lawrence's Church, with its magnificent medieval stained-glass window of Hilda. There has been a church on this site for around 1200 years. The first record dates from AD737, when King Ceolwulf of Northumbria gave the church and village to the abbot and monks of Lindisfarne. Warkworth Hermitage is an unusual relic, situated on the north bank of the River Coquet. It consists of an outer portion built of stone and an inner portion hewn from the steep rock above the river. This inner part comprises a chapel and a smaller chamber, both having altars. There is an altar-tomb with a female effigy in the chapel. Ferries to it across the river are available one or two days a week.
- Hartlepool: Visit St Hilda's Church as described above.
- Marske: Tradition says that Hilda stopped here on her way to Whitby. Visit the church and pray on the shore.
- Whitby: See above.

Bibliography

Primary sources

Annales Cambriae (Castle Studies Research, 2007)

Bede, *Ecclesiastical History of the English People*, Judith Maclure and Roger Collins (eds) (Oxford University Press, 2005)

Colgrave, Bertram (trans.), *The Earliest Life of Gregory the Great* (Cambridge University Press, 1985)

Stephanus Eddius and Bertram Colgrave, *The Life of Bishop Wilfrid* (Cambridge University Press, 1985)

Nennius, *The History of the Britons* (Kessinger Publishing, 2004)

Savage, H.E., 'Abbess Hilda's First Religious House', *Archaeologia Aeliana* Vol. 19 (1898)

Swanton, M.J. (ed.), *Anglo-Saxon Chronicle* (University of Exeter Press, 1996)

Thompson, A.H., 'The Monastic Settlement at Hackness', *Yorkshire Archaeological Journal* Vol. 27, 1924

Warner, Peter, *The Origins of Suffolk* (Manchester, 1996)

'On the Monasteries of S. Hieu and S. Hild', *Yorkshire Archaeological Journal* Vol. 3 (1873)

Secondary sources

Blair, Hunter, 'Whitby as a centre of learning in the seventh century', in Michael Lapidge and Helmut Gneuss (eds), *Learning and Literature in Anglo-Saxon England* (Cambridge University Press, 2010)

Fell, Christine, 'Hild, Abbess of Streonaeshalch', *Hagiography and Medieval Literature: A Symposium* (Odense, 1981)

Fell, Christine, *Women in Anglo-Saxon England and the Impact of 1066* (British Museum Publications, 1984)

Marsden, John, *Northanymbre Saga: The history of the Anglo-Saxon kings of Northumbria* (Llanerch, 1995)

McCash, June Hall, *The Life of Saint Audrey: A text by Marie de France* (McFarland & Company, 2006).

Myres, J.N.L., *The English Settlements* (The Oxford History of England) (Clarendon Press, 1986).

Thornbury, Emily, *Anglo-Saxon England* Vol. 36 (Cambridge University Press, 2007), published online at www.journals.cambridge.org/ase

Wormald, Patrick, *The Times of Bede: Studies in early English Christian society and its historian* (Blackwell, 2006), pp. 614–680 (Appendix on 'Hilda, Saint and Scholar')

Worship resources for the celebration of Hilda

Celtic Daily Prayer: Prayers and readings from the Northumbria Community (HarperCollins, 2002).

Simpson, Ray, *Liturgies from Lindisfarne: Prayers and services for the pilgrimage of life* (Kevin Mayhew, 2010)

Simpson, Ray, *The Celtic Prayer Book, Volume 4: Great Celtic Christians* (Kevin Mayhew, 2004)

The Celtic Hymnbook (Kevin Mayhew, 2004), Nos 8, 22, 44, 88, 165

For some online resources, including hymns, see www.raysimpson.org/resources/downloads or www.aidanandhilda.org

Glossary of places

- **Bernicia**: The most northern Anglo-Saxon kingdom, with its headquarters at Bamburgh. The territory was roughly equivalent to the English counties of Tees, Durham, Northumberland, Lancashire and Cumbria and the former Scottish counties of Berwickshire and East Lothian, stretching from the Forth to the Tees. In the early seventh century, it merged with its southern neighbour, Deira, to form the kingdom of Northumbria. Its borders subsequently expanded considerably to include Dumfries, for example.
- **Dalriada (or Dál Riata)**: The Irish kingdom of Dalriada, in the north or Ireland, colonised an area on the western coast of Scotland (then Pictland), which took the same name. In the late sixth and early seventh centuries it encompassed roughly the area that is now Argyll and Bute and Lochaber in Scotland and also County Antrim in Ireland. It was Christian and encompassed the monastery of Iona. Furthermore, it had a treaty with Northumbrian royal exiles.
- **Deira**: An Anglo-Saxon kingdom in northern England that extended from the River Humber to the Tees, roughly the area of Yorkshire. It was the more southern of the two kingdoms of Deira and Bernicia, which later merged to form the kingdom of Northumbria.
- **Eboracum**: The Roman name for York, perhaps the second most important city of Britain in Anglo-Saxon times.
- **Kingdom of the East Angles**: Roughly equivalent to today's Norfolk, Suffolk and part of Cambridgeshire.

- **Kingdom of the East Saxons**: Roughly equivalent to today's Essex.
- **Kingdom of Lindsey**: Roughly equivalent to today's Lincolnshire.
- **Kingdom of Mercia**: The powerful Anglo-Saxon kingdom in the area of today's English Midlands.

Notes

1 The ninth-century historian Nennius records these. See John Morris (ed.), *Arthurian Period Sources Vol 8: Nennius* (Phillimore, 1998).

2 Tom Holland, *In the Shadow of the Sword: The battle for global empire and the end of the ancient world* (Little, Brown, 2012).

3 Scholars such as J.N.L. Myres argue that King Ceretic of Wessex, from whom King Alfred was descended, was of Celtic origin. See Myres, *The English Settlements* (Clarendon Press, 1986).

4 Solveig Flugstad, in a note to the author.

5 Ray Simpson, *The Celtic Prayer Book, Volume Four: Great Celtic Christians* (Kevin Mayhew, 2004), pp. 63–94.

6 Joan Chittister, *Illuminated Life: Monastic Wisdom for Seekers of Light* (Orbis, 2000)

7 Thomas Taylor, *The Life of St Samson of Dol* (Kessinger Publishing, LLC, 2007).

8 Bede, *Ecclesiastical History* Book I, Ch. 29. York would probably have become home to an archbishop if King Edwin hadn't died in battle in about 633. His death saw Paulinus flee to Kent with Edwin's queen. One of Paulinus's companions, James the Deacon, apparently remained in York but the bishop's seat moved to Lindisfarne in Northumberland. The bishopric was restored in York by the first synod which was held at Whitby in 664. In 735 York did finally became an archbishopric, when Egbert became the first northern Archbishop. Later, Archbishop Ethelberht built Holy Wisdom church, said to be magnificent: unfortunately, its location is unclear. Writings by Bede and Alcuin reveal that York was by now a city of churches. It is thought that a monastic precinct had been created in Bishophill, within which there were several churches.

9 Brian Hope-Taylor, *Yeavering: An Anglo-British centre of early Northumbria* (English Heritage, 2010)

10 *Treatise on the Apostolic Tradition*, often attributed to Hippolytus.

11 Stephen Allott (trans.), *Alcuin of York, c.AD732 to 804: His life and letters* (William Sessions, 1974).

12 Christine Fell, 'Hild, Abbess of Streonaeshalch' in *Hagiography and Medieval Literature: A Symposium* (Odense, 1981).

13 Ray Simpson, *Exploring Celtic Spirituality* (Kevin Mayhew, 2004).

14 Andrew Jones, *Pilgrimage: The journey to remembering our story* (BRF, 2011)

15 Some scholars think that Ethelric was the same person as King Anna's son Egric, who died in 636. Hunter Blair believes that Hereswith was King Anna's sister-in-law and that, around the time when she married into the East Anglian royal family, Anna had already been king for a decade. See 'Whitby as a centre of learning in the seventh century', Hunter Blair, in Michael Lapidge and Helmut Gneuss (eds), *Learning and Literature in Anglo-Saxon England* (Cambridge University Press, 2010).

16 Peter Warner, *The Origins of Suffolk* (Manchester University Press, 1996), pp. 115–118.

17 A twelfth-century, three-volume English chronicle and history, written in Latin at Ely Abbey.

18 June Hall McCash, *The Life of Saint Audrey: A text by Marie de France* (McFarland, 2006).

19 Aleksandar Hemon, *The Book of My Lives* (Picador, 2013).

20 From Juliet Boobbyer and Joanna Sciortino, *Columba: A play with music* (Gracewing, 1981).

21 Julia McGuiness, 'Reflections on life's road', from *The Aidan Way* No. 12 (1997).

22 In John Marsden, *Northanhymbre Saga: The history of the Anglo-Saxon kings of Northumbria* (Llanerch, 1995), p. 112. Later Welsh sources even portray him as arriving with one or two monks.

23 See Fell, in 'Hild, Abbess of Streonaeshalch'.

24 Working title: *Aidan of Lindisfarne: Irish Flame that warms the world*.

25 *Archaeologia Aeliana*, Vol. 17, p. 205 (journal of The Society of Antiquaries of Newcastle upon Tyne).

26 Oswy's victory owed something to the support he received from Dalriada: Penda's death is as widely recorded in the Irish Annals as Oswald's victory over Cadwallon. Oswy's links with Columba's tribe, the Ui Neill, were longstanding. Through an Ui Neill princess, he had fathered a son, Aldfrith, who would one day succeed him on Northumbria's throne. Iona remained faithful and solid in its support. Bishop Finan, whom Iona sent to replace Aidan, was himself the son

of the northern Ui Neill high king, and thus the brother of Oswy's former wife or mistress.

27 Count de Montalembert, *The Monks of the West* Vol. 2 (1872), p. 261.

28 Aetla's name does not appear in any of the lists of bishops. There is no other evidence that a see of Dorchester existed at this time, except for the statement of Florence of Worcester to the effect that a fivefold division of the Mercian diocese took place in 679, that Dorchester was included in Mercia, and that Aetla was appointed as its bishop. The most probable explanation is that a see was established about 679 at Dorchester (which may have been under Mercia at the time) and that Aetla was its bishop but that it had only a very short existence.

29 A late hagiography, the *Vita Sanctae Elfledae*, survives, collected in John Capgrave's *Nova Legenda Anglie*.

30 Marie de France, *Life of St Audrey*, translated and edited by June Hall McCash and Judith Clark Barban (McFarland, 2006), lines 889–915.

31 As a result of this appointment, Cedd is generally listed among the bishops of London.

32 We recall that Wilfrid had caught Queen Enfleda's eye and she had become his patron. She sent him to Canterbury, to the Kentish court, from where he eventually travelled to Rome. When he returned to England in about 658, Oswy's and Enfleda's son, Alchfrith, expelled the Irish monks from their monastery at Ripon and presented it to Wilfrid. Wilfrid was, in short, a young man in a hurry.

33 Eddius Stephanus, *Vita Sancti Wilfrithi* (*Life of St Wilfrid*), written in the early eighth century.

34 Irenaeus, *Against Heresies*, Bk 3, ch. 24.

35 Pope John Paul II, *Ut Unum Sint* ('On commitment to Ecumenism'), encyclical of 25 May 1995.

36 The title of a book by former Chief Rabbi Jonathan Sacks.

37 Quoted from Ray Simpson, *Exploring Celtic Spirituality*.

38 Quoted in A.M. Allchin, *Mission and Transfiguration* (Fairacres Publication No. 44).

39 Wendy Ward, letter to the author.

40 In *Anglo-Saxon England*, Vol. 36 (Cambridge University Press, 2007). The series is now published online at www.journals.cambridge.org/ase

41 Bertram Colgrave (ed.), *The Earliest Life of Gregory the Great* (Cambridge University Press, 1985).
42 In his Introduction to Adrian Whittaker (ed.), *BeGlad: An Incredible String Band Compendium* (Helter Skelter, 2013).
43 Andy Freeman and Pete Greig, *Punk Monk: The ancient art of breathing* (Kingsway, 2007), pp. 139–140.
44 'The poetry is in the pity', from war poet Wildred Owen's 'Preface' to his poems.
45 From Ray Simpson, *The Celtic Prayer Book Vol. 4: Great Celtic Christians* (Kevin Mayhew, 2004).
46 From *Celtic Daily Prayer: Inspirationsal prayer & readings from the Northumbria Community* (Collins, 2005).
47 From Simpson, *Celtic Prayer Book Vol. 4*.
48 Ray Simpson, *Before We Say Goodbye: Preparing for a good death* (Kevin Mayhew, 2001).
49 David Rollason, Conrad Leyser and Hannah Williams (eds), *England and the Continent in the Tenth Century: Studies in honour of Wilhelm Levison* (Brepols, 2010).
50 Christine Fell, *Women in Anglo-Saxon England and the Impact of 1066* (British Museum Publications, 1984), pp. 110–111.
51 www.mowatch.org.au/archives/MOWatch_quiet_day_materials_2012.pdf
52 Prayer by Penny Barnet.
53 This book was transferred to Durham and was continually supplemented by entries made in the tenth century and later. The second section of this list contains 198 names of abbesses, including Hilda's successors at Whitby, Enfleda and Elfleda, and names thought to correspond to those on the memorial stones at Hartlepool, including Hildigyd, Hildidryd, Beorhtgyd and Oedilburga—the abbess of Hilda's daughter monastery at Hackness, who is named on a memorial stone there.
54 Rosalin Barker, *The Whitby Sisters: A Chronicle of the Order of the Holy Paraclete 1915–2000* (Order of the Holy Paraclete, 2001).
55 I am indebted to Anglo-Saxon scholar Paul Cavill for this information.
56 A 16th-century entry in a 15th-century Durham manuscript contains an account of the miracle of Hilda and her snakes. It appears to have been written as a homily and ends with a prayer. William Camden, in

the book *Britannia* (1586), stated, 'If you break ammonites you find within stony serpents, wreathed up in circles, but eternally without heads'. With this legend in mind, Victorian geologists named one local species after Hilda: the ammonite *hildoceras*. Today Whitby's coat of arms (visible at the centre of the swing bridge) also displays three of St Hilda's ammonites.

57 See www.freshexpressions.org.uk/stories/gothchurchcoventry.

58 Quoted by Patsy McGarry, *The Irish Times* (1 November 2013).